The Greatest

SECRET

Ever Told

The Greatest Secret Ever Told

Frank Gerald Steyn, DPhil

© 2017

ISBN-13: 978-1543297843
ISBN-10: 1543297846

Printed by CreateSpace
An Amazon.com Company

Dr. Frank Gerald Steyn
sieketrooster@gmail.com

This Book is Written for All.

The message is for You:
Christian, Muslim, Hindu,
New Age, Unaffiliated, Baha'i,
Buddhist, Atheist, Theist, Deist,
Non-Conformist, Liberal, Moderate,
Humanist, Non-Denominational,
And all who need to delight in the
Belief and Experience of a
Worthy Lifestyle on Earth,
Redemption and Healing,
Hope for the future, and a
Readiness for eternity.

"Go therefore and make disciples of all the nations,
baptizing them in the name of the Father and of the Son
and of the Holy Spirit, teaching them to observe all
things that I have commanded you; and lo, I am with
you always, even to the end of the age." Amen.
Matthew 28:19 and 20

At the Cross of Jesus

It is not the color of your skin…
But the color of your heart.

It is not your language…
But your words of acceptance.

It is not your culture…
But your belief in Christ.

It is not the latest fashions…
But the robe of Jesus' righteousness.

It is not money or poverty…
But the richness of God's grace.

The Greatest Secret Ever Told

Contents

1

Secrets and Mysteries

Colossians 2:2
"My goal is that your hearts would be encouraged and united together in love so that you might have all the riches of assurance that come with understanding, so that you all might have the knowledge of the secret plan of God, namely Christ."

A young person recently said "You can't hand us a latte and then go about business as usual and expect us to stick around. We're not leaving the church because we don't find the cool factor there; we're leaving the church because we don't find Jesus there. Like every generation before ours, deep down, we long for Jesus."

We are living today as always with the world full of individuals who are sinners and in desperate need of God's grace. We are all like broken pottery, but we serve a God who is in the business of mending our damaged personalities, hurt egos, and broken lives. Understanding how vulnerable we are helps us to more effectively grasp and respond to God's grace. This also makes us more genuine and open to face the hopes, heartaches and hurts of those around us with decency and authenticity. God's mercy, kindness and favor makes this possible. This has been a big lesson and an ongoing growing experience for many of us.

Through the past decades my wife and I have served the Lord faithfully and because of our fields of interest, have also been invited to many different Christian churches from Reformed to Apostolic, for seminars, concerts, weekend retreats and training. As a Protestant Christian pastor with years of Theology and Religious studies, seven years as adjunct professor of World Religions and Sociology, we have many times pondered what other persons think about our church. For my Masters research, it was a privilege and joy to use data from 23 Protestant denominations, and for my Doctors thesis, 12 Protestant denominations. We also had the opportunity to visit Hindu Temples, the beautiful white marble Baha'i Lotus Flower in Delhi, as well as a Muslim Mosque. We were also amazed with the beauty and riches of Saint Peter's Cathedral in Rome, climbed up the steps with pilgrims, and were amazed at the marble and beauty. Many windows of learning were opened to, as well as many doors to other churches, including presenting at camp meetings, one-day and weekend seminars and retreats.

What we all need to learn is that we must get our attitude and message in line with the amazing grace of the Lord Jesus, as well as our witness to the increasingly sophisticated populations wherever we share the Gospel. The medium is the message, which means that you are the message.

With people's minds permeated with global cyber and digital technology, including thousands of advertising messages and countless other bits of information vying for a piece of our brains and souls every single day, our Gospel mission is not getting any easier. The avenues to our souls are paralyzed by too much wrong and unsolicited messages, misinformation, snake-oil, greed, television, junk, and advertisers fighting for a part of our brains, and a world that wants to control our lives.

In the following pages, there are some examples that show how easy it is to fall into a frame of mind where we mistakenly place our faith and hopes on wrong bits and bytes of information. One example we heard during a recent church conference in San Antonio, where we heard a number of pastors refer to a six-day Creation week. I always thought that the Creation week of creation was seven days when God created time, space, matter and energy for all on this Earth.

The Creation Museum in Kentucky teaches a six-day Creation, but in honest teaching and evangelism we need to be authentic in that the Bible teaches a seven-day Creation. This make our sharing easier and more effectual as we reveal God's Word, his Sabbath of rest and salvation, within an authentic contextual basis. Jesus says in the New Testament that the "Sabbath was made for mankind," and we need to demonstrate his teachings. At the end of Creation, God's final act was to reveal the first institution that was made holy. He sanctified the Sabbath day, the seventh and final day of the Creation week.

It is easy for fallible humans to fall into a trap, and evil has set many traps for Christians. Many also fall into unwitting traps because the beliefs of other religions and churches have been hammered into their minds. Even forms and theories of evolution easily find ways to get into the human mind. Our lives are often controlled by what we learn. Liberal examples and new philosophies of sexuality are not only increasing in all lands of the world, but also find their way on to hallowed ground.

The Holy Scriptures open the way for understanding and contextualizing our lives. Ask yourself the question 'am I going be genuine, honest and real' when it comes to Bible study? Many folks merely repeat what they have read in a book or heard from someone, and then become 'regurgitators,' but we all need to have a daily spiritual walk with God's Word, by reading pondering, and prayer.

There is an actual, factual and truthful event that has been concealed, confused, denigrated and distorted by humanity for thousands of years, but is at the same time probably the most valuable information that we have ever needed. This event has been maligned, misrepresented and embellished to the extent that the majority of a deceived world has been kept from knowing the vital missing dimension to resolving mankind's problems. Even scientists, theologians, educators and philosophers have remained ignorant of the truth and why humankind really exists. Yet this awesome truth, this incredible knowledge, has always been available.

At the opposite end of the scale there are many, especially Christians, who know about this thrilling mystery, but it has never become a driving centrality and motivation in their lives.

The Hour to Advance Has Manifestly Come

"In every religious movement there come times when the call of God to advance is sounded - a summons to quicken the pace, to take higher ground, to break with the status quo, to enter into a new relationship and experience with Him. Especially is this true in the new Space Age into which we have now entered, with its stupendous achievements.

AN HOUR OF VITAL DECISION - We have clearly come to such a time in the Advent Movement. God has been laying a similar burden upon hearts all over the world. He has implanted a divine restlessness, an anticipation, and a longing that must and will be met. He is impelling men to seek out, and to find and follow His will and way. He is constraining many to study into our backgrounds, that we may understand as never before the way He has led in our early formative years, that the great basic issues of the consummation, and the underlying principles and purposes of God for us today, may be more clearly recognized and followed.

The resultant vision is becoming clearer and clearer, and the divine call sharper, more distinct, and insistent. It is taking on the proportions of a clarion summons. And along with it comes a sobering corollary.

No one ever comes face to face with such a confrontation and remains the same thereafter. When light comes, he either advances in and with that light, or darksome shadows begin to envelop him. The old attitudes and easy momentum of yesteryear are no longer possible. The present is surely developing into such an hour of decision, a time for renewal and advance." *Movement of Destiny*, Leroy Edwin Froom, page 25, Review and Herald Publishing Association, Washington DC, 1971.

This is the reason why God chose to send the Messiah.

Many of us have been programmed, encoded and mesmerized by 'snake oil' purveyors. Many churches do not have pulpits anymore, but stages to excite, hypnotize and entertain. Christ came as Savior and Revealer of the eternal gospel that He declared and demonstrated, and how it involves you!

The statement by Professor Froom is included because we are again living in crucial times. The world is crumbling. Societies are fighting. Economies are failing. People are leaving the Christian Church. Dr. Leroy Froom has a powerful relevant message for all of us.

There are millions of people who know about the true Creator God and what His plans are for all humankind, but it has never really touched their hearts and driven their lives. Many Christians have some cognizant knowledge, but have never delighted in a genuine, real, balanced, heartfelt and personal walk with God.

Gregory Nazianzen, a 6th century church leader and theologian, said about the crucifixion of Jesus: "Many indeed are the wondrous happenings of that time: God hanging from a cross, the sun made dark and again flaming out; for it was fitting that creation should mourn with its creator. The temple veil rent, blood and water flowing from his side: the one as from a man, the other as from what was above man; the earth shaken, the rocks shattered because of the rock; the dead risen to bear witness to the final and universal resurrection of the dead. The happenings at the sepulcher and after the sepulcher, who can fittingly recount them? Yet no one of them can be compared to the miracle of my salvation. A few drops of blood renew the whole world, and do for all men what the rennet does for the milk: joining us and binding us together." (*On the Holy Pasch*, Oration 45.1)

In the following chapters the goal is to look deeper into the secrets and mysteries of God's Word. You will find that there is an amazing connection between Creation (events in Eden) and Jesus' crucifixion on Calvary. There is a vital living relationship and close correlation with the early Biblical teachings in the book of Genesis, the Old Testament Torah, Writings, Psalms and Prophecies, the New Testament Gospels, the letters of the Apostles Paul and John, and the book of Revelation.

This takes us all the way from Eden to Calvary to Eternity. The Word of God uses Promises, Covenants, Prophecies, Parables, Miracles, Types and Power to lead His Remnant through all the centuries.

Opening new windows in understanding Bible teachings should not discourage us or weaken our faith. Reading our Bibles, prayer, study, research, group study, topical study or verse by verse in one chapter, all leads to a deeper understanding of God's Word. You will also better comprehend the awe of Jesus' Love Letter, the Bible. Enjoying time each day to be immersed in the joy and freedom of the Scriptures, will not only help your spiritual growth, but will help you to more efficiently share the amazing truths that we have held on to for so long.

"We have many lessons to learn, and many, many to unlearn. God and heaven alone are infallible. Those who think that they will never have to give up a cherished view, never have occasion to change an opinion, will be disappointed." E.G, White, *Selected Messages Book 1*, p. 416

1 Timothy 3:16

"Without question, the mystery of Godliness is great: God was revealed as a human, declared righteous by the Spirit, seen by angels, preached throughout the nations, believed in around the world, and taken up in glory."

2

Seven Days of Miracles

*"Let the cross of Christ be made the science of all education,
The center of all teaching and all study. Let it be brought
into the daily experience in practical life."*
E.G. White, *The Ministry of Healing*, p. 460

"Measure twice and cut once."

This is good advice a carpenter gave me years ago, that has helped me to make as few mistakes as possible when cutting lumber or metal. There is an old Yiddish proverb that says "Measure ten times and then cut once," which seems to be even more obsessive, and even a little bit fanatical.

The fact is that good workers try to make no mistakes, so they double-check their measurements for accuracy before cutting. They need to be logical and sure of their dimensions and handiwork. Humankind has always been interested in exact measurements and efficient validations.

Some workers compromise, such as a building contractor who told me that if you cannot see something wrong such as a wall an inch off, from twenty feet away, then it is okay. For many of us, that really is not good enough, especially when it comes to the life and mission that God has given me for my life.

Genesis 1 and 2 - Many Christians have a fuzzy idea about what the Bible teaches and can fall prey to any fabrication that comes along. For example, some people believe that the Biblical creation week was six days long, and other persons accept that the process of creating this Earth went through a long process of evolution over millions of years. What is the truth?

Adding to the confusion about the creation week, is the fact that by far the majority of contemporary Christians around the world attend church services on Sunday, the first day of the week. The next largest group, Muslims, have as their special time on the sixth day or Friday. These man-made traditions and human legalism has had the effect of weakening belief in the authenticity of the seven-day creation week. It also opens the way for false beliefs such as the ever-changing theories of evolution that fill the cranial spaces of many minds.

Some liberal scholars teach that the question of whether the seven days of creation were literal days, or symbolic of longer stages of development, is essentially irrelevant to the acceptance of a Creator God. The observable universe, the Earth beneath our feet, and every one of us, exist. Who needs more proof than that? The result is that Christian evolutionary traditions do away with the literal seventh-day

Sabbath, which is a very clear teaching in the Word of God. They even do away with the concept of sin and open the way to more mistakes in our lives. This opens the way to our contemporary secular humanist society.

Some years ago, we were at a monthly group study with pastors from different churches. The Irish priest, Father Murphy from the Roman Catholic Church, surprised some of us when he revealed that: "The theory of evolution has done away with original sin. There was no Adam or Eve. I only baptize babies because it is my job."

Some teach the mistaken doctrine that a person is born sinful and guilty of sin, because of Adam and Eve transgressing in the Garden of Eden. This is shocking news, but does not shake us. We believe that the Bible teaches that at birth, we are not sinners, but rather that we are born with inherent propensities to weakness and sin. Only as you get older and are exposed to the world, sin is a personal willful choice to break the law of God. It is part of our physical heritage and DNA.

Isaiah 64:6 "We are all infected and impure with sin. When we display our righteous deeds, they are nothing but filthy rags. Like autumn leaves, we wither and fall, and our sins sweep us away like the wind."

Also, read John 3:16 and 17.

Christian beliefs and theology have endured many decades and centuries of being twisted, mishandlings, misinterpretations, manipulations and outright lies. The truth is that theories and teachings of evolution do not have any place in Genesis history. The first two chapters of the Bible teach that this Earth and all on it were originally created by the power and order of a caring Lord God. God created time, space, energy and matter. The final two chapters in the Bible, Revelation, proclaim a New Earth and a New Jerusalem. According to Isaiah, the Sabbath will still be enjoyed in the New Earth.

Seven Day Christians - A prayerful reading of the book of Genesis makes it clear that God's Creation of this Earth lasted seven days, and that He rested on the seventh day. This was thousands of years before there were any Jews.

- Genesis 2:2, 3 "And **on the seventh day** (*of the Creation week*) God ended His work which He had done, and He rested **on the seventh day** from all His work which He had done. Then God blessed **the seventh day** and sanctified it, because in it He rested from all His work which God had created and made." *New King James Version*. The Greek Septuagint or LXX translation of the Hebrew Bible reads **Seventh day**, in the Greek Old Testament by Symmachus, the Syriac translation in Aramaic, and the Masoretic Hebrew text, all use the word **'seventh.'**

- Exodus 20:8-11 "**Remember the Sabbath day** and treat it as holy. Six days you may work and do all your tasks, but the seventh day (*of the Creation week*) is a **Sabbath to the Lord your God**. Do not do any work on it—not you, your sons or daughters, your male or female servants, your animals, or the immigrant who is living with you. Because the Lord made the heavens and the earth, the sea, and everything that is in them in six days, but **rested on the seventh day**. That is why the Lord blessed the Sabbath day and made it holy."

- Mark 2:27, 28 "Then he said to them, "The **Sabbath was made** for man, not man for the Sabbath. So the Son of Man is Lord even of the Sabbath."
- Hebrews 4:4 "Then somewhere he said this about the **seventh day of creation**: God rested on the seventh day from all his works."

The seventh day Sabbath is part of creation. These references clearly show that not only was the total creation week seven days long, but also that the Seventh day is the Biblical day of rest (the word *Sabbath* means rest), first enjoyed by God, Adam and Eve. This was thousands of years before the first Jew, Hebrew or Israelite. God created everything, including time and space for this Earth, for all people.

"The weekly cycle of seven literal days, six for labor and the seventh for rest, which has been preserved and brought down through Bible history, originated in the great facts of the first seven days." E.G. White *The Great Controversy*, Chapter 8.

Sabbath is a rehearsal for Eternity.
While we are living in this present
time of Jesus' Kingdom of Grace,
it is a day of faith and mercy. Behavior
or works cannot save us, but God
through His grace offers us the Seventh
Day as a day of rest, remembrance and
celebration, and a day of worship.

"On the seventh day of the first week GOD rested from his work, and then blessed the day of his rest, and set it apart for the use of man. The weekly cycle of seven literal days, six for labor, and, the seventh for rest, which has been preserved and brought down through Bible history, originated in the great facts of the first seven days." E. G. White, *Basic Statement on Geology*, 1864

The Adventist church is at the forefront when it comes to the authentic Lord's Day, the seventh day of the Creation Week. It is not the Jewish Sabbath. Adam and Eve, Noah, Abraham, Isaac and Jacob were not Jews. The name of God's 'chosen people' as 'Jews' was a much later event. Contemporary history shows that even modern Jewish persons largely do not respect the Bible Sabbath anymore.

The following is a refreshing look at the spiritual significance of the seventh day Sabbath that comes from the pen of the late Rabbi Aryeh Kaplan of New York City, *"Sabbath - Day of Eternity"* (Mesorab Mafitzim, Jerusalem, 1974). "On the Sabbath, G-d created Harmony between Himself and the universe. When man observes the Sabbath, he too partakes of G-d's eternity. He enters into a state of harmony with both G-d and the world. Man is then in a state of peace with all creation. This immediately explains why the concept of peace is so important on the Sabbath. One of the most common Sabbath greetings is Shabbat Shalom/Sabbath peace, for the main idea of the Sabbath is peace; not just peace between man and his fellow, but peace between man and all creation."

The fourth Commandment in Exodus 20:8-11 reads: "Remember the Sabbath day and treat it as holy. Six days you may work and do all your tasks, but the seventh day is a Sabbath to the Lord your God. Do not do any work on it - not you, your sons or daughters, your male or female servants, your animals, or the immigrant who is living with you. Because the Lord made the heavens and the earth, the sea, and everything that is in them in six days, but rested on the seventh day. That is why the Lord blessed the Sabbath day and made it holy." This substantiates that our Earth was created in seven days. God worked at forming the Earth for six days and then rested on the seventh day of Creation. We are also reminded to work six days, and then enjoy the seventh day as a Sabbath of rest.

It is said that the Sabbath is a rehearsal for eternity. While we are living on this side of eternity, it is also a day of grace. Behavior, legalism and works cannot save you, but God through His grace offers us the seventh day as a free gift, a day of rest, remembrance and celebration.

Just as many original Bible doctrines have been forgotten and remain a mystery to many people, the true Creation Sabbath has been forgotten. In fact, the Sabbath commandment in the Decalogue begins with the work *'Remember.'*

The Sabbath More Fully - The founder of the Moody Bible Institute wrote, "Sabbath was binding in Eden, and it has been in force ever since. This fourth commandment begins with the word 'remember,' showing that the Sabbath already existed when God wrote the law on the tables of stone at Sinai. How can men claim that this one commandment has been done away with when they will admit that the other nine are still binding?" D.L. Moody, Weighed and Wanting, page 47.

Sabbath is a relationship with God. How can we keep both sane and faithful in this hectic, confusing, technological, mind-boggling and cyber-spaced world? How can we cope with so many people around us who are overwhelmed by anger, frustration, fretting, and the frenzy of the rat race? We all need time out. One of God's greatest gifts to us is the Sabbath, a day of rest, gladness and celebration. The seventh-day Sabbath is rooted deep in God's way for our lives. The deep spiritual meanings and relevance of the Biblical Sabbath is important for each of us. We do not keep the Sabbath. The Sabbath keeps us. We have a graceful, merciful and loving God who wants us to live a happy balanced life.

It is the premise of this book that the Sabbath can be shared more fully only in the light of the seven-day creation week. Anything less than this takes away the significance, validity, fullness, substance, and meaning of God's day of rest.

The fullness, joy and freedom of God's Sabbath can only be fully comprehended in the light of the Cross of Calvary.

Jesus is the Sabbath more fully.

We do not keep the Sabbath.

The Sabbath keeps us.

3

Promise of Redemption

*"I will put contempt between you and the woman,
between your offspring and hers. They will strike
your head, but you will strike at their heels."*
Genesis 3:15

An amazing fact of nature that has intrigued me for many years, is that there are mathematical certainties and unwavering outcomes that by themselves contradict the many theories of evolution. There is order and discipline in nature, and not much because of chance.

As far as we know, there are a limited number of basic chemical elements. Up to this point in time, just more than 120 have been discovered. While there must be more elements that have not been found yet, the basic elements remain the same. Iron (Fe) atoms found on Earth are identical to iron atoms found on meteorites. The iron atoms in the red soil of Mars are also identical.

These are the building blocks of our universe. Each element has an amazing story of its own, with practical benefits of every element known to science, from helium-neon lasers to luminous radium watch dials. There are different methodologies for listing the elements, including by atomic number or number of atoms, atomic mass, electron configuration, number of neutrons, melting point, boiling point, or crystal structure.

Scientific formulations and research with microelectronic microscopes show that the laws regarding basic structures of atoms, the elements and DNA, are invariable and do not permit exceptions.

There is order in nature.

There is order in Biblical Creation.

There is order in the seven-day weekly cycle.

There is also order in the Bible, the Word of God.

There is order in Bible prophecies, including the Old Testament prophecies that point to the Cross of Calvary. In the Old Testament, there are more than four hundred prophetic indications of the coming of the Messiah, fulfilled by the Son of God, the Lord Jesus Christ.

This brings us to the first prophecy in the Scriptures. In the third chapter of Genesis, after the account of Creation, and after sin reared its ugly head in the early days of human history, God reveals the rebellious fallen Lucifer as a serpent. After sin entered this Earth in the form of Satan and those he tempted, these prophetic words came from God as found in Genesis 3:15, "I will put contempt between you and the woman, between your offspring (זֶרַע *zera`* *meaning semen, offspring, seed*) and hers. They will strike your head, but you will strike at their heels."

When God created our Earth and all on it, there was no sin. The terrible reality of sin began when Lucifer together with one third of the angels was cast out of the heavenly courts because of his rebelliousness, power hunger and disloyalty to God. Satan then proceeded to tempt Adam and Eve into doubting God and perpetrating the first sin.

The context of these words in Genesis 3:15 is the fall into rebelliousness of Adam and Eve. God is speaking to the serpent who was a disguise of Satan. God draws a distinction between 'your seed' (Satan's seed) and 'her Seed' (the Messiah). *Her Seed* refers to the incarnation and humanity of Jesus Christ. Notice that this passage does not say that the 'seed' was of Adam. This is an inference to the virgin birth. In Galatians 3:16, the New Testament calls Jesus the 'Seed.'

Genesis 3:15 is understood as prophetic of Satan's attempt to destroy the Son of God and His redemptive work, but in the end Christ will completely crush his head and obliterate the existence of the rebellious Devil. The arch enemy is hard at work defaming, deceiving, denigrating, destroying and demolishing the Love and Grace of God. Satan will try to take away the joy we have in following Jesus in our lives, as well as enjoying the fellowship of His church on Sabbath morning. We need to remember that our rest and salvation is only in the Lord and Savior Jesus.

After the original appalling, soul-breaking sinfulness, God had at least three choices. He could have destroyed all and started all over again, but this would indicate failure.

Secondly, God could have forced our first ancestors to be virtuous without the ability to choose for themselves, but only do his bidding. This choice was not selected, because it would have meant that God created robotic creatures, and not warm-hearted feeling humans with the ability to make their own choices.

Thirdly, God had the choice of extending His grace, allowing the human race to carry on through all the millennia of the history of the present Earth. He would then send his only Son, Jesus, to enter the sinful environment that we live in, to show that the first Adam did not have to sin. His Son would then become the sin offering and sacrifice on the Cross of Calvary. This reveals God's love, grace, mercy and hope that our Lord has for each of us. Read Romans 5:12 and 23, "Just as through one human being sin came into the world, and death came through sin, so death has come to everyone, since everyone has sinned... The wages that sin pays are death, but God's gift is eternal life in Christ Jesus our Lord."

Grace now rules.

The reference in the New Testament to the word *seed* is found in Galatians 3:16 "The promises were spoken to Abraham and to his seed (σπέρμα *sperma* meaning semen, seed, children, or offspring). Scripture does not say "and to seeds," meaning many people, but "and to your seed," meaning one person, who is Christ."

Even at the moment of the first sin and rebellion, God promised a solution to their sin. At the fall, Satan bruised the heel of Jesus. Sin was the cause of Christ going to the Cross, but the Cross of Jesus Christ crushed Satan's head. One is a non-lethal, and the other a lethal, act. At the cross Jesus dealt Satan a fatal blow. There Jesus fully paid for the penalty of sin. God predicts the defeat of Satan by the first advent of Jesus Christ, the Messiah. "He shall bruise your head" is a mortal wound. The power of Satan is crushed by the Cross of Christ. Now we are free to come to Jesus, the Lamb of God pleading for us with his blood. We were saved more than 2,000 years ago. All any person is invited to do now, is to accept this free gift of pardon, salvation and new life.

Christ not only paid for the sins of the world on the Cross, but he triumphed over Satan there: Colossians 2:14, "He destroyed the record of the debt (IOU) we owed, with its requirements that worked against us. He canceled it by nailing it to the cross."

"And you shall bruise His heel" refers to the death of Christ. Whether this refers literally to the heels of Jesus pressed against the cross, is not important. Jesus was bruised at the cross. This first prophecy in Genesis 3:15 sets the stage for the rest of the Word of God, the history, prophecies, promises, Gospels, and the Blood of Our Savior Jesus that permeates all the Old and new Testaments. Read Isaiah 53.

Even though the Ten Commandments did not exist engraved on stone yet, as far as Adam and Eve were concerned, their choice to believe the lies of Satan was still a rebellion and sin. In the same way, the seventh-day Sabbath was not there as a written law. Our early ancestors realized that what God said and gave to them at Creation, was important and a law in their hearts.

Similarly, the Ten Commandments did not exist on tables of stone when Cain killed his brother Able, but it was still sinful to murder, because God's way was in their hearts.

Because of sin in the Garden of Eden, every human being has inherited built-in tainted DNA and inherits the consequences of being born with the propensity to sin. We are all born into a sinful family. We all have all inherited weakness and perverted tendencies resulting from sin. We are all subject to death. A baby is not born guilty of original sin, but is born with the propensity to sin as they get older.

God is in no way unfair, but has provided a plan to have our sins forgiven and our lives cleansed by the Blood of Jesus, who was the supreme sacrifice on the Cross of Calvary. Together with the account of the creation of a sin-free Earth, and then the fall into sin because of the wiles of Satan, God gives us a way out, Jesus' death on the Cross.

John 3:16 and 17 "God so loved the world that he gave his only Son, so that everyone who believes in him won't perish but will have eternal life. God didn't send his Son into the world to judge the world, but that the world might be saved through him."

Following is a timeline or summary of what God has done for us. There are three key verses in the Bible that have the word '*beginning*' in its introduction.

Genesis 1:1 "In the beginning God created the Heavens and the Earth."

Mark 1:1 "The beginning of the gospel of Jesus Christ, the Son of God."

John 1:1 and 2 "In the beginning was the Word and the Word was with God and the Word was God. The same was in the beginning with God."

To re-arrange the sequence and timeline of the events in these three verses, we can do the following:

1. Chronologically John 1:1 comes first. Jesus Christ, our Lord and Savior, was there and pre-existent with His Father at the creation of this Earth. He is the Creator.
2. Genesis 1:1 reveals the initial creation of our planet Earth. Genesis 1:2 says "The earth was without form,

and void; and darkness was on the face of the deep. And the Spirit of God was hovering over the face of the waters." Together with what John 1:1-2 and the rest of what the Bible declares, this is evidence that validates God as one in three persons, but completely united as One Deity, the Father, the Son and the Holy Spirit.

3. Mark 1:1 tells us about the beginning of the Gospel and then Mark goes on to reveal the life, ministry and death of Jesus. Jesus initiates a new Covenant, the Covenant of Grace, sealed with His Blood.

This brings us back to Genesis 3:15, which in the Old Testament prophetically announces redemption, and the in the New Testament Gospels the fulfillment is the Cross of Jesus Christ.

The next step in the narrative, is YOU.

After crowds were baptized, new churches were organized, and the Gospel of Grace went through the whole world, all the way to this generation that you belong to – where do you stand? Just close your eyes and visualize walking to the Cross. You kneel there, confess and then tell the Lord "Take my life and let it be consecrated Lord to Thee."

"The cross of Christ brings us nigh to God, reconciling man to
God, and God to man. Without the cross, there is no means
provided for overcoming the power of our strong foe.
Every hope of the race hangs upon the cross.
When the sinner reaches the cross, and looks up to the
One who died to save him, he may rejoice with fullness of joy;
For his sins are pardoned. Kneeling at the cross,
He has reached the highest place to which man can attain."
E.G. White, *Our High Calling*, p. 46

At the Cross...

At the cross,
At the cross where
I first saw the light,
And the burden of my
Heart rolled away,
It was there by faith
I received my sight,
And now I am
Happy all the day!
Isaac Watts

4

God's Hidden Mysteries!

"So a person should think about us this way –
as servants of Christ and managers of God's mysteries.
In this kind of situation, what is expected of a
manager is that they prove to be faithful"
1 Corinthians 4:1, 2

The internet throbs with impending destruction, meteor strikes, global war, climate change or other cataclysmic events. What will happen soon? What is predicted to happen? Who will destroy Planet Earth?

All over this Earth there are Christians who believe that we are living in the last days of history as we know it. Many preachers and writers proclaim that the world is entering its darkest hour and morally regressing into the same state as ancient Sodom and Gomorrah.

Conspiracy theorists are predicting a meteor or comet will hit the oceans causing massive tsunamis and ruin.

Even objective Bible words such as Apocalypse and Armageddon are misused to strike fear into our hearts.

It seems as if our world has become just a giant village spreading rumors and scary stories for itching ears and eager listeners hungry for escape, instant gratification, entertainment, stimulation, catastrophe and cataclysm. Is this mass hysteria? The prophetic words of 1 Timothy 3:1-4 are relevant to the time we are living in: "Understand that the last days will be dangerous times. People will be selfish and love money. They will be the kind of people who brag and who are proud. They will slander others, and they will be disobedient to their parents. They will be ungrateful, unholy, unloving, contrary, and critical. They will be without self-control and brutal, and they won't love what is good. They will be people who are disloyal, reckless, and conceited. They will love pleasure instead of loving God."

The BBC's *End Day* program is a TV show that comes back every few years with new docudramas and scenarios of impending doom and destruction. Mostly five scenes of the last days on planet Earth are presented. These involve nuclear destruction, meteor impacts, volcanic eruptions, pandemics, earthquakes, or CERN'S Large Hadron Collider destroying the world.

But we are often in denial and seek mental and emotional escapes. Despite increasing scares, threats, natural destruction, murder and mayhem, cable news programs often dish up entertainment, sport, the latest pop music, or other distractions in an effort to lull our minds. It feels as if people are fiddling while the world burns, escaping to drink, drugs and entertainment.

At the same time, there is a great hunger in the hearts of men and women. There is a need for deeper understanding of the world that we are living in. We need a closer spiritual walk with our Creator, Lord and Savior. One of our greatest needs is just to be able to live balanced lives and the ability to see world events in the perspectives of Bible promises and prophecy.

More than ever before, we need to fully embrace Jesus' sacrifice on the Cross of Calvary is the center of the Bible, of history, and of our lives and homes. The Blood of our Messiah the Lord Jesus flows through all of the Word of God like a scarlet thread from Genesis to Revelation.

The Enigmatic Isaiah 28:10 - New understanding and discoveries in the Word of God should not lead us to deviate from our faith, but rather lead us to enjoy deeper Christian maturity. The Holy Spirit can lead us to deeper understanding, spiritual growth and humility each day. When we pray, read and study earnestly, we often find that well-known older interpretations can be seen in more depth. We have all come across themes and messages that we feel could be more proficiently and powerfully proclaimed.

A fascinating example is Isaiah 28:10 and 13 "For precept *must be* upon precept, precept upon precept; line upon line, line upon line; here a little, *and* there a little." King James Version.

The following Scriptures are shared without trying to be dogmatic or fanatic. Read these Biblical statements as they appear in different versions and translations. For ease and efficiency, we will only use verse 10 of Isaiah 28 as it is repeated in verse 13. The best method that we can use as we study the Scriptures is Bible Theology, or studying the Word of God by researching the Bible itself. Compare different translations and versions, including the original languages. Carefully read the chapter or context.

This differs from Systematic Theology, which looks at notable authors and scholars for guidance in interpreting the Scriptures. Systematic Theology and Biblical Criticism led one professor of Theology at the end of the year to hold up the empty covers of his Bible, and proclaim "Now this is all we have left..."

Following are some versions and translations of **Isaiah 28:10**.

- **Hebrew:** *"Tsav latsav tsav latsav / kav lakav kav lakav"* In reading the original text it turns out that these are not actual grammatical Hebraic words, but are just nonsense sounds that babies may use. Just like *blah, blah, blah.*
- **1611 King James Version**: "For precept *must be* upon precept, precept upon precept; line upon line, line upon line; here a little, *and* there a little:"
- **1978 New International Version**: "For it is: Do this, do that, a rule for this, a rule for that; a little here, a little there." (*Foot note*: probably meaningless sounds mimicking the prophet's words)
- **1983 Afrikaans** (my home language) "Wat ons van hom hoor, is 'n bietjie brabbeltaal hier en 'n bietjie brabbeltaal daar!" (*Direct Translation*: All we hear from them is babble talk, some babble talk.)
- **2011 Common English Bible**: It is "tsav letsav, tsav lestav; qav leqav, qav leqav, a little of this, a little of that." (*Foot Note*: A Hebrew version of baby talk or

gibberish) This Bible edition is one of the first honest translations of the Hebrew text.

— **Bible dictionaries** explain the Hebrew non-word *tsav* as used as a sound in mocking mimicry of Isaiah's words, and thus not a true divine command. The next Hebrew word is *kav,* also an unclear and meaningless sound.

The context of Isaiah 28 reveals that God's followers are in an infantile, immature, childish, mesmerized state and do not hear the actual message that God has for them. Verse 7: "These also stagger from wine and stumble from beer: priest and prophet stagger from beer; they are confused by wine; they stray on account of beer; they err when receiving visions; they stumble when making judgments." This sounds like Revelation 3:17 "You say, 'I am rich. I have everything I want. I don't need a thing!' And you don't realize that you are wretched and miserable and poor and blind and naked."

What does Isaiah really say? This is God telling us about the great human escape. "You are in denial. You misuse your time, mind, hearts and energies with TV entertainment, sport, computers, cell phones, tablets, drugs and drunkenness and worldly things. You forget all about me."

From Muttering to Integrity: The meaning of God's message through the prophet Isaiah is summarized later in chapter 28:16, 17 "Therefore, the LORD God says: Look! I'm laying in Zion a stone, a tested stone, a valuable cornerstone, a sure foundation: the one who trusts won't tremble. I will make justice the measuring line and righteousness the plumb line."

It was a great learning experience for me, when a lady invited me to their home to meet her son. She did not say much, but she took me down the passage to her son's bedroom. There this 35-year-old man was lying in a large baby cradle with sides. He seemed fully grown, but the painful truth was that here was a man with a properly developed body, but the brain of a 3-month old baby. He had to be bottle and teaspoon fed, washed and cleaned. He could not care for himself. His brain never developed,

This touched my heart, to see a grown man who was just a big baby. But I have also met full-grown 'Christian' men and women, fully mature physically, but stunted spiritually. This is what Isaiah and the Apostle Paul describe in the Scriptures.

In summary, Isaiah 28:10 says "You must grow up, leave the bottle, throw away your pacifier, get rid of your security blanket, you should not need diapers any more, get rid of your training wheels – and stand up, step out, grow in Jesus, and enjoy a growing daily experience of healing, joy and grace in Jesus."

In the New Testament, the Apostle Paul testifies to the same observation and our need to grow in maturity and grace. Where there is no development, Paul writes in 1 Corinthians 3:2: "I have fed you with milk, and not with meat: for hitherto ye were not able to bear it, neither yet now are ye able." Hebrews 5:11-14 "We have a lot to say about this topic, and it's difficult to explain, because you have been lazy and you haven't been listening. Although you should have been teachers by now, you need someone to teach you an introduction to the basics about God's message. You have come to the place where you need milk instead of solid food. Everyone who lives on milk is not used to the word of righteousness, because they are babies. But solid food is for the mature, whose senses are trained by practice to distinguish between good and evil." CEB

Following is a summary and context of Isaiah's message.

Summary of Isaiah 28 – Some of the Israelites had returned to the Holy Land from captivity. They were very busy in establishing new lives, but neglected God and their spiritual lives were stunted. They were mature adults, but acted like little babies when it came to their relationship with God. They have never grown up.

The prophet Haggai in chapter 1 puts it this way: "So now, this is what the LORD of heavenly forces says: Take your ways to heart. You have sown much, but it has brought little. You eat, but there's not enough to satisfy. You drink, but not enough to get drunk. There is clothing, but not enough to keep warm. Anyone earning wages puts those wages into a bag with holes." Haggai 1:5 and 6.

It seems that Christians globally have mistranslated, misguided, and fostered an inaccurate message from Isaiah 28:10. It does not say *for precept must be upon precept, precept upon precept; line upon line, line upon line; here a little,* and *there a little* (KJV). This may be a shock to you, but being immersed by the Holy Spirit speaking to your heart, the message of this verse can lead to a profounder relationship with the Deity. The problem is that even the insightful and beautiful language of the King James Version does have some slipups.

For modern Christians, a deeper understanding of Isaiah 28:10 and 13 does not only mean a radical change in the way that we study the Scriptures, but is rather a challenge to dig deeper and enjoy more genuine growth for our lives in this strange new cyber world.

God's message can be either terror or salvation, but our God offers calm, peace, balance and a good night's sleep.

People's minds are often filled with trivia and sometimes God has to speak to us in baby language.

Isaiah 28:23 "Listen and hear my voice; pay attention and hear my word."

The message for contemporary Christians waiting for the Advent sounds like God saying: 'You have done well encouraging people to live healthy, eat well and stop drugs and smoking. You have done a good job with your schools, hospitals and preaching prophecy. The whole world now has health shops, vegetarians and vegan eating. More than 75% of all people do not smoke any more. Now I exhort you to enjoy a deeper heart and mind relationship with Me.' In verse 16 God says "Look! I am laying in Zion a stone, a tested stone, a valuable cornerstone, a sure foundation: the one who trusts won't tremble."

Proclaim the Lord Jesus and His Cross. Help people not only to live healthy and work hard, but to come to the Cross of the Messiah and enjoy a new deeper spiritual life. We also need more valid and deeper methods of Bible study. There is nothing wrong with line upon line, but more meaningful and deeper reading, study and sharing in groups are also imperative.

In summary, Isaiah 28:10 says "You must grow up, leave the bottle, throw away your pacifier, get rid of your security blanket, you should not need diapers any more, get rid of your training wheels – and stand up, step out, grow in Jesus, and enjoy a growing daily experience of healing, joy and grace in Jesus."

Hebrews 5:11-14 "We have a lot to say about this topic, and it's difficult to explain, because you have been lazy and you haven't been listening. Although you should have been teachers by now, you need someone to teach you an introduction to the basics about God's message. You have come to the place where you need milk instead of solid food. Everyone who lives on milk is not used to the word of righteousness, because they are babies. But solid food is for the mature, whose senses are trained by practice to distinguish between good and evil."

The nonsensical gobbledygook words of Isaiah 28:10 and 13 may also describe some of us as individuals. We often come across folks that say that they feel as if they have no meaning on Earth. Their lives are empty, hollow and without motivation or any real purpose. It is *"tsav letsav, tsav lestav; qav leqav, qav leqav, a little of this, a little of that."*

Just as we have found that these words in Isaiah 28:10, 13 have no meaning and do not occur in Hebrew Lexicons, many people feel as if their life has no meaning. Life is senseless, meaningless, powerless, normless and has no excitement or ideals. Like a speedboat going in circles but not getting anywhere. Our lives need to be more like a great ocean going ship, with goals, purpose and outcomes.

For many men and women, the daily tedium is getting up, drinking coffee, going to work, coming home, watching TV, going to bed, getting up, drinking coffee, going to work... Life is meaningless emotionally, physically and mentally.

What God is telling us through the prophet Isaiah, is that we can change, be forgiven, enjoy new life and new lifestyles. We need to go deeper. Maybe our lives need replanting or the need of a good life coach.

Try your church.

Call your pastor.

Speak to someone.

Grow up.

A challenge from the pen of the Apostle Paul in Ephesians 4:13-16 reads "God's goal is for us to become mature adults - to be fully grown, measured by the standard of the fullness of Christ. As a result, we aren't supposed to be infants any longer who can be tossed and blown around by every wind that comes from teaching with deceitful scheming and the tricks people play to deliberately mislead others. Instead, by speaking the truth with love, let's grow in every way into Christ, who is the head."

Many people live secret lives. They are unhappy and do not know where to turn. Some hide their anxiety, bitterness, pain and loneliness for years. Feelings of hurt and disappointment remain hidden from parents, friends, spouses and colleagues for years. Nothing seems wrong, per se, but the unhappiness gets worse and worse. Many persons with the most beautiful smiles are sad and feel hurt and lonely inside. It takes a lot of practice to hide things so that all seems normal, but inside their head and heart they are bleeding.

"One of the most tragic things I know about human nature is that all of us tend to put off living. We dream of some magical rose garden over the horizon - instead of enjoying the roses that are blooming outside our window today." Dale Carnegie

It is almost an oversimplification to say that it all starts in the home where we grow up. Our family of origin is significant, important, crucial, vital and the very basis of our whole make-up, personality, temperament and soul. For many centuries it was called the basic building block of society – but these days the family is crumbling, attacked, dysfunctional and nearly obliterated. Many folks come into life without a moral compass.

Just the same as you get dysfunctional families, there are also dysfunctional churches, congregations or groups. On the island of Patmos, the Apostle John writes in Revelation 3:20, in the message to the Church at Laodicea that Jesus is knocking on the door. In chapters 2 and 3 we find God's message to these seven churches – and pictures the Lord Jesus as knocking on the door of the Laodicean or final Church in history.

Our only hope is to be reborn, start all over again. Grow and mature each new day. The Cross of Jesus makes this possible. Also open the door of your heart.

"Hanging upon the cross Christ was the gospel. This is our message, our argument, our doctrine, our warning to the impenitent, our encouragement for the sorrowing, and the hope of every believer. Paul's confession, "For me to live is Christ," is said to be the most perfect interpretation in a few words, in all the Scriptures, of what it means to be a Christian. This is the whole truth of the gospel." E. G. White, *The Desire of Ages*, page 211.

All the teachings, narratives, miracles, prophecies, salvation history, and invitations of the Word or God, our Bible, are centered in Jesus as Lord, Creator and Redeemer.

Jesus At the Center - *Israel Houghton*
Jesus be the center of my life
Jesus be the center of my life
From beginning to the end
It will always be, it's always been You
Jesus, Jesus

Mighty
God

Creator

Peace

Sabbath
of Grace

Jesus

Lord
of
Lords

Savior

King of
Kings

5

The Key That Unlocks Secrets

Isaiah 64:4 (700 BC)
"From ancient times, no one has heard,
No ear has perceived, no eye has seen any god but you
Who acts on behalf of those who wait for him!"

The prophetic words of Isaiah 64:4 in the Old Testament present a mystery with a key and solution, which has essentially been neglected by many people for thousands of years. These poetic words are like a trumpet-call preceding an imperative gospel message that will change our hearts and lives.

Isaiah lived around seven hundred years before Jesus, and is well known as the Messianic prophet of the Old Testament. The words of Isaiah 64:4 are repeated by the Apostle Paul in 1 Corinthians 2:9, demonstrating that Isaiah's prophetic words were fulfilled, but not all readers understand what this vital message really involves.

There is a mystery that has clouded and obscured our perception and meaning of Isaiah 64:4, and as repeated by Paul in 1 Corinthians 2:9. Most readers have understood that these poetic words describe heaven. The message of these texts is not about heaven as commonly understood.

We are certain that both Isaiah (*the Messianic prophet*), and Paul (*The Apostle of Jesus Christ Crucifi*ed), in their hearts and because of life experiences, knew what the core message meant. When you read the contexts of Isaiah and Paul, we find that these words are both a prophecy and fulfillment of the coming Messiah and His sacrificial crucifixion. Paul declares: "For I determined not to know anything among you, save Jesus Christ, and him crucified." 1 Corinthians 2:2. This is the grand theme of Paul in all his letters to the seven New Testament churches.

What is the key to many Biblical queries?

The Key is Jesus!

"The cross of Calvary challenges, and will finally vanquish every earthly and hellish power. In the cross all influence centers, and from it all influence goes forth. It is the great center of attraction; for on it Christ gave up His life for the human race." E.G. White, *Lift Him Up*, p. 230

Much of our world has been misled and blinded from knowing the vital missing dimension to resolving mankind's problems. Scientists, theologians, educators and philosophers have remained ignorant of the real certainties of why humankind really exists, and what God has prepared for those who love him. And yet, this awesome truth, this incredible knowledge, has always been available, but most have not known where to look.

Christ came as Savior, as well as Revealer of future events, explaining in advance good news for all mankind. This is the amazing story of the phenomenal good news that He brought, and how it involves you!

The gospel of Jesus and redemption has been cheapened by discounted teachings grace and the superficial study of the story of redemption.

- Can world religions hold the secret plan of God back?
- What is the greatest, most significant event in the history of the universe?
- What are the details of God's grand redemptive plan?
- What does the Word of God say about this great mystery and secret?
- What is the awesome potential of your life?

Our lives are often spiritually stunted, reserved, restrained, repressed and we hold back, but from the time we let go and let God, there is no limit to our healing, growth and spiritual maturity. From the time we let God, through the power of the Holy Spirit and the blood of Jesus, remove the obstacles that are inhibiting our emotional, mental, and physical growth and maturity, we enjoy new life, vibrant spirituality, and better relationships.

In the book of Isaiah, the Messianic prophet identifies the coming Messiah as a Servant and how he cares for Israel. From chapter 51 Isaiah prefigures the Messiah as the Redeemer and Restorer of Zion. In chapters 63 and 64, we find Isaiah's prayer and yearning of the people for the Messiah, Savior and Shepherd.

It is with this context and meaning that that the author expresses the enigmatic words in 64:4 "From ancient times, no one has heard, no ear has perceived, no eye has seen any god but you who acts on behalf of those who wait for him." These words are repeated verbatim by Paul in 1 Corinthians 2:9.

Paul's content does not mention the word *heaven* anywhere in 1 Corinthians 2, therefore invalidating the meaning that is commonly associated with this verse. This epistle starts in chapter 1 by Paul identifying Jesus as Lord and Savior. He then writes about God's faithfulness and grace.

We also find Paul's key to the understanding of his theology in 1 Corinthians 1:17 and 18 - "Christ did not send me to baptize but to preach the good news. And Christ did not send me to preach the good news with clever words so that Christ's cross won't be emptied of its meaning. The message of the cross is foolishness to those who are being destroyed. But it is the power of God for those of us who are being saved." These amazing words are central to each one of Paul's letters, in his conversion on the Damascus Road, in his life and ministry and in 1 Corinthians chapter 2.

In chapter 2:1, 2 he writes "When I came to you, brothers and sisters, I did not come preaching God's secrets to you like I was an expert in speech or wisdom. I had made up my mind not to think about anything while I was with you except Jesus Christ, and to preach him as crucified."

1 Corinthians 2:7 and 8 "We talk about God's wisdom, which has been hidden as a secret. God determined this wisdom in advance, before time began, for our glory. It is a wisdom that none of the present-day rulers have understood, because if they did understand it, they would never have crucified the Lord of glory!" And then the crucial key to God's wisdom and mysteries:

1 Corinthians 2:9 "But this is precisely what is written: God has prepared things for those who love him

- *that no eye has seen,*
- *or ear has heard,*
- *or that haven't crossed the mind of any human being.*"

The Cross of Calvary where our Savior was killed, dying for our sins, has tremendous meaning for each of us. We need to grow up and leave our breast-fed days behind, and feast on what God has for each exciting new day.

There is a story of a visitor to Yosemite National Park asking one of the guides, "If you only have one hour to see Yosemite, what would you do?" The ranger said, "Madam, if I only had one hour to see Yosemite, I would sit on that rock down there and cry for an hour."

God's beautiful nature is the heart of Yosemite. Touring the valleys, forests and trails, the impressive waterfalls, Half Dome, and the High Sierra, we enjoy nature as never before. There is so much beauty, time to rest and ponder all that God has given to us.

We witnessed something similar at Niagara Falls. About half of the tourists near us at the falls had their thumbs on their cellphones. We can spend a lot of time and money on the mundane and trifles, without getting to the central purpose and meaning of our lives.

The Word of God is like that. You need to spend a lot more than a few minutes or one hour per day to enjoy the vistas, glory and the ups and downs of mankind and nations. Meditating on the Word of God is a good plan to unlock the secrets and mysteries that the Creator wants us to make part of our very souls.

The awesome truth is that our Lord has already made it all possible for us. His marvelous and amazing grace preceded our lives. God put in place a plan way back in the Garden of Eden when our first parents sinned, and then affirmed it 2,000 years ago, on a hill called Calvary, when His Only Son died on a cruel cross for our redemption.

This plan including the blood of Jesus our Savior is here right now, waiting for your faith, trust and acceptance. Despite our brokenness, God calls each person and makes it possible for us to choose to follow a just and merciful God. Remember that Jesus prayed for all, and tears ran down his face for you, as he spent an agonizing night in the Garden of Gethsemane.

God's Whisper in Our Hearts

Deuteronomy 31:8 "The Lord is the one who goes ahead of you; he will be with you. He will not fail you or forsake you. Do not fear, or be dismayed."

God knew you and prepared many signposts leading to salvation, even before you knew yourself. This is called prevenient grace. After going through a list of people who died in faith, Paul says in Hebrews 11:39, 40 "All these people did not receive what was promised, though they were given approval for their faith. God provided something better for us so they wouldn't be made perfect without us."

Thus, prevenient grace is that grace which goes before, and is antecedent to human action. J. B. Moody expresses this thought this way: "Grace reigned not only in the past eternity in contriving the plan, but also in time in executing it, and will continue to reign till consummated. It is from everlasting to everlasting. Hence grace reigned in our redemption, regeneration, justification, sanctification, and will reign in our preservation, resurrection and ultimate glorification." *The Exceeding Riches of the Manifold Grace of God*, p. 166. Hall-Moody Institute, Martin, Tennessee.

Prevenient grace is the grace, love and mercy that God has prepared for all of us, all the way from Adam and Eve. You will find many markers in your life that you did not even know that led you to new life in Jesus. God has a plan for your life, even if you were born and bred in a bad part of town. You can change for the better.

This grace was already predicted in Genesis 3:15

There are many doctors, lawyers, teachers and preachers that grew up in bad neighborhoods – but accepted their lives and circumstances as a challenge. They saw that there is good that endures in society. God has, in each of our lives, the earnest longing for change and deliverance from sin, meaninglessness and death, and this leads to repentance and faith. The Godhead already prepared our salvation since the rebellion in the Garden of Eden. The coming of the Messiah and His sacrificial death on the Cross of Calvary is identified as such an amazing event, that it is prophetically and in real life, an inexpressible event:

E. G. White, *The Ministry of Healing*, pp. 473, 474. "Often our plans fail that God's plans for us may succeed. In the future life the mysteries that here have annoyed and disappointed us will be made plain. We shall see that our seemingly unanswered prayers and disappointed hopes have been among our greatest blessings."

As we progress to the New Testament we find the prophetic words of the Messianic prophet Isaiah repeated by the Gospel missionary and preacher, the apostle Paul.

1 *Corinthians* 2:9 (67 AD) *"But this is precisely what is written: God has prepared things for those who love him that no eye has seen, or ear has heard, or that haven't crossed the mind of any human being."*

The newest state-of-the-art technological security improvements use biometric checking to make sure that you are you. These include visual systems to look at your eye, iris, retina and the patterns of veins in the back of the eye; visually identifying your ears to check the shape; and the chemical biometrics of an individual using the analysis of segments from their DNA.

The Word of God has been down to earth and up to date for a long time.

Each new day.

For each new soul.

For each new individual.

God knows us inside out, all of us.

Jesus said: "Truly I tell you, unless you change and become like little children, you will never enter the kingdom of heaven." Matthew 18:3 (NIV)

In 1 Corinthians 2:9 we find that God's challenge is for our faith and belief to be founded on measures even more advanced than scientific reasoning using eyes, ears and the human brain. The understanding and insight of this statement can only be portrayed by looking at the clarity and simplicity of the Gospel of Jesus and the Cross.

God's voice and wisdom is not found in lofty statements or impressive promises, but in a still small voice... He said, "Go out, and stand on the mountain before the LORD." And behold, the LORD passed by, and a great and strong wind tore into the mountains and broke the rocks in pieces before the LORD, but the LORD was not in the wind; and after the wind an earthquake, but the LORD was not in the earthquake; and after the earthquake a fire, but the LORD was not in the fire; and after the fire a still small voice." 1 Kings 19:11 and 12. (NKJV)

As in Isaiah 64:4 that Paul quotes, this is a good description of God's grace for all on Earth. Long before any of us had been born and given life on this Earth, God already had plans in place for our redemption. This goes all the way back to the Garden of Eden and can be read in Genesis 3:15. This is the first prophecy in God's Word: "I will put contempt between you and the woman, between your offspring and hers. They will strike your head, but you will strike at their heels." This is mostly understood as Satan wanting to destroy the Son of God and His redemptive work, but in the end Christ will completely crush his head and terminate the existence of the rebellious Devil.

Genesis 3:15 is the first indication and promise in the expansive vista of Bible prophecy. Here we find the crimson thread of the Cross of Jesus Christ that runs through the whole of God's Word, Old and New Testaments.

In much of the Christian world we are told that 1 Corinthians 2:9 refers to 'Heaven', but in searching the context closely, we find that Paul is not speaking about heaven, and that the word *heaven* is not even found in that chapter of 1 Corinthians 2 at all.

Paul begins this chapter by writing in verses 1 and 2 "When I came to you, brothers and sisters, I didn't come preaching God's secrets to you like I was an expert in speech or wisdom. I had made up my mind not to think about anything while I was with you except Jesus Christ, and to preach him as crucified." This develops as Paul's pivotal, imperative, urgent, deep and heartfelt message in each of his letters sent to seven New Testament Churches.

The Bible tells us that there are things that God has prepared for those who love him and wait for him. There are things prepared in a future life for Christians, things that just human sense cannot discover, no present information can convey to our ears, nor can yet enter our hearts. We need all of this plus the miracles of grace and mercy, so that life and immortality can be brought to eternity through the gospel. 2 Timothy 1:10 "Now his grace is revealed through the appearance of our Savior, Christ Jesus. He destroyed death and brought life and immortality into clear focus through the good news."

The apostle speaks here of the divine gospel miracle for each of our lives. These are such as eye has not seen nor ear heard. By simple observation and using only empirical methods, the great truths of the gospel are things lying out of the sphere of human discovery: *"Eye hath not seen, nor ear heard them, nor have they entered into the heart of man."*

"Were they objects of sense, could they be discovered by an eye of reason, and communicated by the ear to the mind, as matters of common human knowledge may, there had been no need of a revelation. But, lying out of the sphere of nature, we cannot discover them but by the light of revelation. And therefore we must take them as they appear in the scriptures, and as God has been pleased to reveal them." Matthew Henry, *Commentary on 1 Corinthians 2*. Public Domain. The accidents and traumas of life could lead us away, cloud and drug our minds – but the Lord Jesus through His blood, and the power of the Holy Spirit, offers you new life.

"I pray that the eyes of your heart will have enough light to see what is the hope of God's call, what is the richness of God's glorious inheritance among believers"
Paul in Ephesians 1:18

The greatest secret ever told, starting in Genesis, to thousands of years later up to the time of Jesus the Messiah, is God our Father sending His Only Son incarnate, to be sacrificed on a cruel Roman cross, so that all humans regardless of culture, race, ethnic group, gender, age or socio-economic status can enjoy free salvation through faith, because of God's amazing grace.

A genuine study of 1 Corinthians 2:9 reveals that these words in the Bible have a primary meaning that reveals truths hidden in the mystery of the Word of God. There are also other meanings, which together with the basic sense, form the core concepts of the Gospel of our Lord Jesus Christ. Following are some of the meanings that we can extrapolate from 1 Corinthians 2:9:

1. These divinely inspired words primarily and essentially refer to the death of Jesus Christ on the cross, both prophetically (Isaiah 64:4) and in implementation (1 Corinthians 2:7-11).

2. They also imply the amazing experience of God's Grace and Redemption in our lives that is so marvelous that we do not always have the words to describe it. The words are not to be limited to future blessings in heaven. They are true of the present and eternity. (Luke 9:23).

3. The end-result of the Cross of Jesus in our lives, the preaching of the Gospel to the whole world, is eternal life in Heaven and the Earth made new. This old life is not all. We do not need the great Jewish festivals or a yearly pilgrimage to Jerusalem. God is now with all who want Him, anywhere on this planet. Wherever you are, alone or lonely, or in a crowd, walking in the woods or on a beach, or driving your car – God is here and now – with you.

Spiritual truths and mysteries are not sufficiently described by things we see or hear, nor by merely using our senses and human methods, but through the power of the Holy Spirit, the power of the Word of God, the power of the blood of Jesus, and the power of prayer and life experiences.

The Lord Jesus understood this fully when he related a real life understanding in Matthew 6:22, 23 "The eye is the lamp of the body. Therefore, if your eye is healthy, your whole body will be full of light. But if your eye is bad, your whole body will be full of darkness. If then the light in you is darkness, how terrible that darkness will be."

We find that it is virtually impossible for any human mind to completely comprehend even one truth or promise of the Holy Scriptures. Deep study and prayer is needed. This is similar to the methodologies and conclusions of any human or natural science. Any research scientist finds out that there is still much more to learn, more to discover, more to forget and more to grasp. We may catch the glory from one point of view, another from another point, yet we can discover only what is basically within our available world view and frame of reference. The complete spectrum and brilliance is often beyond our vision.

It is the same with the Word of God. The same as when you climb to the top of a mountain, only to find that there are more mountains beyond. It is like the ocean, with amazing beauty, breadth and depths that are not easy to fathom. The Word of God opens the way for new vistas, distant horizons, new discoveries, new joys, changed lifestyles, and the discoveries of new secrets about God and ourselves. We also find that the simplicity of a child's understanding, vulnerability, spontaneity, enjoyment of new experiences, openness and honesty, are some of the most important learning methods (Matthew 18:3).

Matthew 13:34, 35
"Listen, my people, to my teaching; tilt your ears toward the words of my mouth. I will open my mouth with a proverb.
I'll declare riddles from days long gone – ones that we've heard and learned about, ones that our ancestors told us."

Why Did Jesus Speak in Parables? The Lord Jesus explained to the crowds why he used parables and what their purpose was "Jesus said all these things to the crowds in parables, and he spoke to them only in parables. This was to fulfill what the prophet spoke: I'll speak in parables; I'll declare what has been hidden since the beginning of the world." Matthew 13:34, 35, Psalm 78:2. As a child, we were taught that 'Parables are Earthly stories with a Heavenly meaning.' This picture has stuck in my mind for a long time.

After the disciples asked Jesus why He used parables, Jesus answers in Matthew 13:13-17, *"This is why I speak to the crowds in parables:*

- *Although they see, they don't really see;*
- *And although they hear,*
- *They don't really listen or understand.*
- *What Isaiah prophesied has become completely true*
- *You will hear, to be sure, but never understand; you will certainly see but never recognize what you are seeing.*
- *For this people's senses have become calloused, and they've become hard of hearing, and they've shut their eyes so that they won't see with their eyes or hear with their ears or understand with their minds, and change their hearts and lives that I may heal them. Happy are your eyes because they see. Happy are your ears because they hear. I assure you that many prophets and righteous people wanted to see what you see and hear what you hear, but they didn't."*

Verses 14 and 15 are a direct reference to Isaiah 6:9, 10 where the prophet emphasizes that God called him to proclaim a message of redemption and renewal. God said,

"Go and say to this people:

- *Listen intently, but don't understand;*
- *look carefully, but don't comprehend.*
- *Make the minds of this people dull.*
- *Make their ears deaf and their eyes blind,*
- *So they can't see with their eyes or hear with their ears,*
- *Or understand with their minds, and turn, and be healed."*

Matthew 13:10 and 11 set the background as to why the Lord used parables: Jesus' disciples came and said to him, "Why do you use parables when you speak to the crowds?

Jesus replied, "Because they haven't received the secrets of the kingdom of heaven, but you have."

At Jesus' Cross, it is not the color of your skin, but the color of your heart. It is not your language, but your words of acceptance. It is not your culture, but your belief in Christ. It is not the latest fashions, but the robe of Jesus' righteousness. It is not money or poverty, but the richness of God's grace. John 3:16 "God so loved the world that he gave his only Son, so that everyone who believes in him won't perish but will have eternal life." The good news of the Gospel of Jesus is that today you can start all over again. Luke 9:23 "Take up your cross daily." Jesus made our new healed hearts and heads possible 2,000 years ago already.

Luke 8:9, 10 "His disciples asked him what this parable meant. He said, "You have been given the mysteries of God's kingdom, but these mysteries come to everyone else in parables so that when they see, they can't see, and when they hear, they can't understand."

It turns out that *Ground Zero* is not the Garden of Eden, Pearl Harbor, New Mexico during the Atom bomb, New York City on 9/11, or anywhere else place on Earth, but on Calvary. This is where your God in agony and grace sent His Only Son for your healing and forgiveness.

Jesus died at ground zero on the Cross of Calvary. Pray the prayer of Daniel and ask for understanding and spiritual guidance, "As I prayed to the Lord my God, I made this confession: Please, my Lord - you are the great and awesome God, the one who keeps the covenant, and truly faithful to all who love him and keep his commands: We have sinned and done wrong. We have brought guilt on ourselves and rebelled, ignoring your commands and your laws. We haven't listened to your servants, the prophets, who spoke in your name to our kings, our leaders, our parents, and to all the land's people. Righteousness belongs to you, my Lord!" Daniel 9:4-7

Hidden: Apart from the Biblical use of the terms secret and mystery, the word *hidden* is also used. The following shows how many times these adjectives are used in the 1611 King James Version and the 2011 Common English Bible:

- *Secret/s*   **KJV** 78   **CEB** 185
- *Mystery/ies*   27   24
- *Hidden*   17   119

An inspiring book of the Bible that we found that also utilizes the word *hidden* is Paul's letter to the Ephesians. In his letter to the Ephesians, the Apostle Paul brings another meaning to the word *hidden*. This epistle strongly emphasizes the experience of the early Christian church, their need of love, their need of reconciliation, and taking the focus off the Jewish Christians only. God through Paul implores the believers to include gentiles or non-Jews in this young church.

Paul writes about the Godhead's plan of sharing the Gospel of Jesus, his grace, faithfulness and love, to all the nations, ethnic and language groups, in the world. Ephesians 1:9 "God revealed his hidden design to us, which is according to his goodwill and the plan that he intended to accomplish through his Son."

In purposefully using the words *'hidden or secret'* Paul refers to God's mysterious or hidden plan of bringing all peoples into the fold of Christianity. Ephesians 3:3-6 "God showed me his secret plan in a revelation, as I mentioned briefly before (*when you read this, you'll understand my insight into the secret plan about Christ*). Earlier generations didn't know this hidden plan that God has now revealed to his holy apostles and prophets through the Spirit. This plan is that the Gentiles would be coheirs and parts of the same body, and that they would share with the Jews in the promises of God in Christ Jesus through the gospel. I became a servant of the gospel because of the grace that God showed me through the exercise of his power. God gave his grace to me, the least of all God's people, to preach the good news about the immeasurable riches of Christ to the Gentiles. God sent me to reveal the secret plan that had been hidden since the beginning of time by God, who created everything."

This includes the fact that God's secret plan is the Cross of Jesus, the Sacrifice of the Son of God and Son of Man, and the forgiveness and cleansing through the Blood of the Lamb - but this plan is also to be extended to all nations, tribes and peoples. Ephesians 4:23-25 "Renew the thinking in your mind by the Spirit and clothe yourself with the new person created according to God's image in justice and true holiness... each of you must tell the truth to your neighbor because we are parts of each other in the same body."

These are important words for the world today. Instead of the United Nations, we have divided nations. More than ever, Daniel's prophecy of the end time, of some strong and many weak nations, has been fulfilled. Global geopolitics of our modern world is succinctly and well defined in Daniel 2, as Daniel's prophetic vision of the end of the world is described. The figure of the man comes to the final prophetic historic period of the feet and toes of iron and clay that do not mix. This is the world that we are living in. Some world nations are strong, but many are weak, and find it difficult to get along, just as iron and clay do not mix.

Some years ago, we bought ice cold soda on a sidewalk in hot and humid Washington DC, and briefly spoke to the African American salesman. He described the USA to us as being the *Melting Pot* and then said "...but maybe this is not a melting pot, because we do not get on with each other."

The more politicians we have, the worse the world is getting. The more lawyers we have, the worse crime statistics are. The more MD's we have, the more people are dying of strange new diseases. The more economists we have, the worse the economy is. The more MBA's we have, the worse labor relations and unrest is becoming. The more theologians we have, the more the modern Laodicean churches are miserable, blind, naked and poor spiritually.

More than ever before, we need to pray and plead for groups to come together. A study on world religions reveals that the only religion where people of all Socio-Economic Status, all classes, rich or poor, all colors, ethnic groups and languages can enjoy membership, is the Seventh-day Adventist Church. Their outreach of mission, hospitals, schools, disaster relief, and churches reach all classes and categories worldwide. This is the model that we need to keep as precious, and constantly keep in our hearts and prayers. This includes more than 20,000,000 members and 30,000,000 plus adherents.

An analysis of data from the 2014 Religious Landscape Study by the Pew Research Center finds that the levels of diversity vary widely within U.S. religious groups. Seventh-day Adventists top the list with a score of 9.1: 37% of adults, meaning that they are the most diverse of religious groups. (http://www.pewforum.org/religious-landscape-study/)

There is another letter to the Ephesians in the New Testament, in the book of Revelation, where the Apostle John writes words of promise, prophecy and condemnation to seven churches in Revelation chapters 2 and 3. In Revelation 2:4, 5 the following message is given to this first out of the seven churches, Ephesus: "I have this against you: you have let go of the love you had at first. So remember the high point from which you have fallen. Change your hearts and lives and do the things you did at first."

John gives a similar message to the church at Ephesus in Ephesians 3:17, 18 "I ask that Christ will live in your hearts through faith. As a result of having strong roots in love, I ask that you'll have the power to grasp love's width and length, height and depth, together with all believers."

Expanding the Gospel Message of the Cross:
The main theme of this book, *The Greatest Secret Ever Told*, is Jesus the Sacrificial Lamb of God, his atoning death on the cruel Roman Cross, and the Gospel of Grace. The Bible also tells us that this Gospel of the Lord Jesus dying for us, the ripping of the Temple curtains in two, brings to fruition not only the end of redemption only for the Jews, but for all people. Ephesians 1:10 "This is what God planned for the climax of all times: to bring all things together in Christ, the things in heaven along with the things on earth. We have also received an inheritance in Christ." Ephesians 3:6 "This plan is that the Gentiles would be coheirs and parts of the same body, and that they would share with the Jews in the promises of God in Christ Jesus through the gospel."

Amen!

Following are verses from Ephesians that use the words *hidden, secret or mystery*. These three words have the same basic meaning in any language, and are translated differently in various Bible versions or translations:

Ephesians 1:9 "God revealed his **hidden** design to us, which is according to his goodwill and the plan that he intended to accomplish through his Son."

Ephesians 3:3-6 "God showed me his **secret** plan in a revelation, as I mentioned briefly before *(when you read this, you'll understand my insight into the **secret** plan about Christ)*. Earlier generations didn't know this **hidden** plan that God has now revealed to his holy apostles and prophets through the Spirit."

Ephesians 3:9, 10 "God sent me to reveal the **secret** plan that had been hidden since the beginning of time by God, who created everything."

Ephesians 5:12, 13 "It's embarrassing to even talk about what certain persons do in **secret**. But everything exposed to the light is revealed by the light." People's private secrets often hide something sinister or evil, but all this will be brought to light in the final judgment.

Ephesians 6:19 "As for me, pray that when I open my mouth, I'll get a message that confidently makes this secret plan of the gospel known." Read Matthew 28:18-20 about the Everlasting Gospel, God's Covenant of Grace for this time, and for all people regardless of ethnicity, race, skin color and language. Isaiah 64:8 *"But now, Lord, you are our father. We are the clay, and you are our potter. All of us are the work of your hand."*

6

Enigmatic and Mysterious Events

"In the sanctuary, the Cross of Christ is the great center of the whole scheme of human redemption. Around it clusters every truth of the Bible. From it radiates light from the beginning to the end of both dispensations. Nor does it stop here. It penetrates the great beyond, and gives the child of faith a glimpse of the glories of the future eternal state. Yea, more than this, is accomplished by the Cross. The love of God is manifest to the universe."
E.G. White, *The Cross and its Shadow*, p. 9

Daniel 8 and 9: The book of the prophet Daniel, chapter 9, has one of the most significant prophecies in the Word of God. The chapter introduces this prophecy with Daniel's fervent and heartfelt prayer for his people. Daniel 9:3 "I then turned my face to my Lord God, asking for an answer with prayer and pleading, and with fasting, mourning clothes, and ashes."

This passionate pleading of Daniel was motivated by the hurt that he felt in his heart for the nation who had turned their backs on the Lord God. This is the prayer from verses 4 to 16.

— *We have sinned and done wrong.*
— *We have brought guilt on ourselves and rebelled,*
— *We have ignored your commands and your laws.*
— *We haven't listened to your servants, the prophets,*
— *We are ashamed this day*
— *We didn't listen to the voice of the LORD our God*
— *All Israel broke your Instruction and turned away*
— *We didn't try to reconcile with the LORD our God*
— *We haven't listened to God's voice.*
— *We have sinned and done the wrong thing.*
— *We have become a disgrace to all our neighbors*

Daniel 9:17-19 continues Daniel's appeal to God: "But now, our God, listen to your servant's prayer and pleas for help. Shine your face on your ruined sanctuary, for your own sake, my Lord. My Lord, listen! My Lord, forgive! My Lord, pay attention and act! Don't delay! My God, do all this for your own sake, because your city and your people are called by your name." During this prayer, while Daniel was still speaking to God, Gabriel came to him in vision.

As an answer to Daniel's passionate prayer, Gabriel said that he had come to deliver a prophetic message to him: "Daniel, here's why I've come: to give you insight and understanding. When you began making your requests, a word went out, and I've come to tell it to you because you are greatly treasured. So now understand this word and grasp the meaning of this vision!" Daniel 9:22, 23

The glory and power of God is amazing. While Daniel was still busy praying, God immediately sent a messenger with the answer to Daniel's supplication and an answer as to the future of God's people.

Daniel and the Scarlet Thread of the Messiah Jesus' Blood

The prophet Daniel lived at an important crossroads of the history of God's people. Daniel 9 outlines the bridge between the Old and the New Testaments, and traces the transition of the world of God's people Israel, and how it was transferred to spiritual Israel in New Testament times. With its fulfilment on the Cross of Calvary to the Day of Pentecost in Acts 1, God's appeal goes out to all peoples, Jew and Gentile, to become part of God's Kingdom of Grace.

The way that this prophecy is revealed to Daniel is spectacular, bringing God's people all the way from the Old Testament, through the New Testament, and all the way to the Apocalypse or Revelation. After Daniel's vision in chapter 8 and prayer in chapter 9:4-14, he was given the vision of the seventy weeks.

The mysteries of God are again revealed, but this time through a prophet. Daniel 9:24 "Seventy weeks are appointed for your people and for your holy city to complete the rebellion, to end sins, to cover over wrongdoing, to bring eternal righteousness, to seal up prophetic vision, and to anoint the most holy place."

Jesus often referred to Old Testament laws and prophecies. He used the historical method for interpreting this vision of Daniel when He announced, "The time is fulfilled, and the kingdom of God is at hand" Mark 1:15. In this affirmation of prophetic fulfillment Jesus Christ alluded to Daniel's 70-week prophecy Daniel 9:24-27, which foretold the appearance of the Messiah.

Near the close of His life Jesus again referred to the same prophecy. This time, however, He pointed to another aspect- to "And after the sixty-two weeks Messiah shall be cut off, but not for Himself; and the people of the prince who is to come shall destroy the city and the sanctuary." Daniel 9:26. Also read Matthew 24:15 and Luke 21:20. These events were to take place after Jesus' death and ascension. Their historical fulfillment occurred in the destruction of Jerusalem and the temple by the Romans in A.D. 70.

Daniel chapters 8 and 9 contain a wealth of information with dates and times, which can be reliably calculated and shown to reveal the exact time of Jesus' first Advent or Coming, the Crucifixion in the middle of the prophetic week, as well as the time when the Gospel will go out to all, including Jews and Gentiles.

The explanation of these prophetic words is given in Daniel 9:24-27. Here is a summary:
- There will be seven weeks from the moment the word went out to restore and rebuild Jerusalem until a leader is anointed.
- And for sixty-two weeks the city will be rebuilt with a courtyard and a moat. But in difficult times.
- After the sixty-two weeks, Messiah will be cut off.

- No one will support him.
- The army of a future leader will destroy the city and the sanctuary.
- His end will come in a flood, but
- Devastations will be decreed until the end of the war.
- For one week, he will make a strong covenant with many people.
- **By the middle of the week, he will stop both sacrifices and offerings. (Crucifixion of Jesus)**
- In their place will be the desolating monstrosities
- Until the decreed destruction sweeps over the devastator.

Daniel 9:27 "By the middle of the week, he will stop both sacrifices and offerings." Christians teach that these prophetic passages predict the exact dates that the Messiah would come and die. The explanation is that Jesus fulfilled these predictions. The traditional date of Jesus' crucifixion is April 33 AD. From this date on, Temple sacrifices and festivals were not needed anymore. Jesus became our Lamb of Sacrifice, the First Fruits, and our Passover.

The centrality and importance of the Cross of Calvary throughout Old Testament prophecies indicates the value that God places on His people. Even though there is a four-hundred-year time period between the Old and New Testaments, the Gospel message, God's way of salvation, is still the same. "Jesus Christ is the same yesterday, today, and forever!" Hebrews 13:8. God always calls His people back to the original eternal Covenant that was first made with Adam and Eve in the Garden of Eden, including the promise of redemption and restoration.

The Sanctuary on Earth and the Sanctuary in Heaven

We read in Psalm 102:19 (NLT) "Tell them the LORD looked down from his heavenly Sanctuary. He looked down to Earth from Heaven."

This is repeated in the New Testament in Hebrews 8:5 (NLT) "They (*the priests*) serve in a system of worship that is only a copy, a shadow of the real one in heaven. For when Moses was getting ready to build the Tabernacle, God gave him this warning: "Be sure that you make everything according to the pattern I have shown you here on the mountain."

We read in the book *The Great Controversy*, Chapter 28, as E.G. White wrote more than 150 years ago: "I was shown a Sanctuary upon earth containing two apartments. It resembled the one in heaven. I was told that it was the earthly Sanctuary, a figure of the heavenly. The furniture of the first apartment of the earthly Sanctuary was like that in the first apartment of the heavenly. The vail was lifted, and I looked into the Holy of Holies, and saw that the furniture was the same as in the Most Holy place of the heavenly Sanctuary. The priests ministered in both apartments of the earthly. In the first apartment he ministered every day in the year, and entered the Most Holy but once in a year, to cleanse it from the sins which had been conveyed there. I saw that Jesus ministered in both apartments of the heavenly Sanctuary. He entered into the heavenly Sanctuary by the offering of his own blood. The earthly priests were removed by death, therefore they could not continue long; but Jesus, I saw, was a priest forever.

Through the sacrifices and offerings brought to the earthly Sanctuary, the children of Israel were to lay hold of the merits of a Savior to come. And in the wisdom of God the particulars of this work were given us that we might look back to them, and understand the work of Jesus in the heavenly Sanctuary."

"At the crucifixion, as Jesus died on Calvary, he cried, 'It is finished', and the vail of the temple was rent in twain, from the top to the bottom. This was to show that the services of the earthly Sanctuary were forever finished, and that God would no more meet with them in their earthly temple, to accept their sacrifices. The blood of Jesus was then shed, which was to be ministered by himself in the heavenly Sanctuary."

The important elements that most interpretations agree with, is that there is a heavenly Sanctuary, and that the Old Testament Sanctuary, Tabernacle, or Temple as it was in Jesus' time, has both prophetic and redemptive verities.

- The Earthly Sanctuary was a copy of the heavenly.
- The Sanctuary and later the Temple was there to give a tangible teaching and demonstration of God's way for our lives.
- Jesus' death on the cruel Roman cross brought an end to the need of sacrifices, the wilderness Sanctuary or Temple.
- When the temple curtain was ripped apart late that Friday afternoon, revealing the Holy Place, it signified that the way to God and salvation does not need priestly and sacrificial intercession anymore. Salvation is now

available to all regardless of race, gender, ethnicity or
skin color. We do not need priests anymore.

- Since the Cross we are living in the time of God's
  Kingdom of Grace. Jesus wants you to accept the
  salvation that he offers, and a new lifestyle in his name.
- Our Lord Jesus is right now in the Heavenly Sanctuary,
  ministering for us on Earth, and preparing for the
  Second Advent.
- The ministry, sacrifice and message of the soon Second
  Coming of the Messiah Jesus that we read about in the
  four NT Gospels, should take hold of our hearts, heads
  and hands.

*"Just as Moses lifted up the snake in the wilderness, so must
the Son of Man be lifted up so that everyone who believes in him
will have eternal life. God so loved the world that he gave his only
Son, so that everyone who believes in him won't perish but will
have eternal life. God didn't send his Son into the world to judge
the world, but that the world might be saved through him."* John
3:14-17

The Torah on Earth and Torah in Heaven.

The Disciples had a unique and very precious
experience when they spent three years sitting at Jesus' feet.
This was an exceptional opportunity to know Jesus as only
these first disciples could know him. What would it be like
to journey back to the first century and sit at the feet of Rabbi
Jesus as one of his disciples? How would your
understanding of the gospel have been shaped by the
customs, beliefs, and traditions of the Jewish culture in
which you lived?

Jesus, the Son of God became fully human and stood at the conflux of two eras. He had to train a dedicated team that would soon oversee establishing the Christian church, of teaching radical (*back to the root meaning*) changes for both Jews and Gentiles. The disciples grew up in a mixed society, but they were mostly trained in Jewish schools and society. Now they are gaining fresh new insights as they listen to their Lord Jesus. It is as if Jesus offered them fresh nurture like rain falling from heaven.

Rain falls from heaven to earth, in a sense, connecting heaven and earth. It is significant that Jewish rabbis compare the Torah to rain falling from heaven to earth: Rabbi Yehudah said, "The day when rain falls is as great as the day when the Torah was given, as it is said in Deuteronomy 32:2 "Pay attention and I will speak; Earth! Listen to the words of my mouth. My teaching will fall like raindrops; my speech will settle like dew - like gentle rains on grass, like spring showers on all that is green - because I proclaim the Lord's name: Give praise to our God!"

When Moses said "teaching," he meant Torah, as it is said of the Torah in Proverbs 4:2 "For I give you sound teaching; do not abandon my Law/Torah" (תּוֹרָה *towrah.*)

Jewish scholars compared Torah to water, for just as water descends from a higher to a lower level, so too, the Torah descended from its place of glory to the realm of men. In Isaiah 55:1 the words of the Torah equate water as "All of you who are thirsty, come to the water!" This is to teach that just as water flows from a higher place to a lower place, so too the words of the Torah descend from a high place to a low place" (*Talmud*).

The Torah in the Old Testament refers to the Jewish *written Law*, consisting of the first five books of the Hebrew Bible, known more commonly as part of the Old Testament, which were given by God to Moses on Mount Sinai, and included all the Biblical laws of Judaism. The Torah is also known as the Chumash, Pentateuch or Five Books of Moses.

The multiple meanings of *Torah* include: A scroll made from kosher animal parchment, with the entire text of the Five Books of Moses written on it; the text of the Five Books of Moses, written in any format; or it can mean the entire corpus of Jewish law. This includes the Written and the Oral Law.

In rabbinic literature, "it was taught that the Torah was one of the six or seven things created prior to the creation of the world. According to Eliezer ben Yose the Galilean, for 974 generations before the creation of the world the Torah lay in God's bosom and joined the ministering angels in song.

Simeon ben Lakish taught that the Torah preceded the world by 2,000 years and was written in black fire upon white fire.

Akiva called the Torah "the precious instrument by which the world was created."

Rav said that God created the world by looking into the Torah as an architect builds a palace by looking into blueprints. It was also taught that God took council with the Torah before He created the world.

Another rabbinical viewpoint is that God created the world for the purpose of revealing the Torah; therefore, since, as the philosophers say, "the first of thought is the end of the work," the Torah is said to have existed before the world. (From *The Jewish Virtual Library – Torah*)

> *"Waters will spring up in the desert, and streams in the*
> *wilderness. The burning sand will become a pool, and*
> *the thirsty ground, fountains of water."* Isaiah 35:6, 7

One more question: is the Old Testament *Torah* (the written law or teachings and instructions) the same as the New Testament *Logos* (word, a saying, doctrine, or teaching)?

From Genesis to the final book of Revelation, the Protestant Christian Bible is a unified library of sixty-six books that essentially agree with each other. The Old Testament was originally written mostly in Hebrew and the New Testament mostly written in Greek. As far as dictionaries, theology and traditional usage go, the two words, Torah and Logos, have:

- Essentially the same meanings
- But also deeper theological implications

Both words infer the written or recorded records, teachings and doctrines, in the Old and New Testaments, but under the New Testament Covenant of Grace these words have the deeper meaning, not only of being written, or taught, but come to life and are humanized in the person of Jesus the Messiah. In other words, during the Jewish period the Torah is truth, and going into the Christian period, the Word or Torah becomes warm blooded, empathic, and filled with grace.

This brings us to the conclusion that the promised Messiah of the Old Testament is fulfilled as the Christ of the New Testament. The prophesied Messiah *(Hebrew)* or Christ *(Greek)* is the incarnated Son of God and the Son of man.

Jesus of the Old Testament is Jesus of the New Testament, and wants to be the Jesus of your heart, home, church, and your soul.

We have seen now that: the Sanctuary on Earth was modelled after the Sanctuary in Heaven;

Jesus of the New Testament was the prophesied Messiah of the Old Testament;

The Torah of the Old Testament became the Word of the New Testament, but the Cross of Calvary was only on Earth! This cruel Roman instrument of torture and death was only on Earth, but the Lord Jesus our Messiah overcame all of this and is ministering in Heaven for you right now.

> *"Men of Galilee," they said, "why are you*
> *standing here staring into heaven?*
> *Jesus has been taken from you into heaven,*
> *but someday he will return from heaven*
> *in the same way you saw him go!"*
> **Acts 1:11**

The Tabernacle and Jesus' Cross

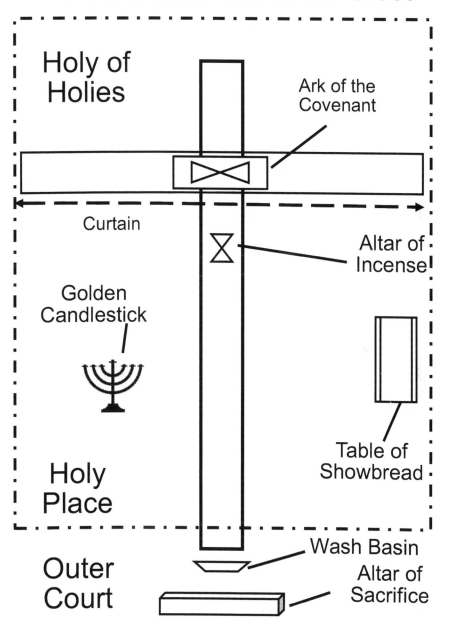

7

An Empty Cross

"It is at the cross of Calvary that mercy and truth meet together, where righteousness and peace kiss each other. The sinner must ever look toward Calvary; and with the simple faith of a little child, he must rest in the merits of Christ, accepting his righteousness and believing in his mercy."
E.G. White, *Materials*, 1888

Many reports and indicators in the media reveal that society is not winning the war on the sustainability of energy, environment and natural resources. There are many warnings of dire outcomes. In one decade, the oceans have lost half of all its fish. Arab, Eastern and Asian regimes are menacing and preparing to attack the west at some future date. Shortages and exploding populations are threating global stability. The next Great War will be triggered by problems with food, water and religious fanaticism. The invasion of legal and illegal immigrants experienced in Europe, the Americas and Southern Africa by mainly Muslim people consists of greater masses of people than the invasions of the early Islamic empires. The volatile status of our world needs the message of God's Word and his grace, the love and salvation that Jesus the Messiah offers, and the guidance of the Holy Spirit more than ever before.

There is a deep historical, philosophical and spiritual foundation in all the writings, history, songs, prayers and poems, prophecies and exhortations of the Bible. The Protestant Christian Scriptures consist of 66 separate books, written by 40 authors, over a period of more than 1,600 years. The amazing fact is that God's message flows through these books with consistency, accuracy, and singleness of aim that you do not find in any other discipline. It is certain that even in physical and natural sciences there is no set of works, over such a period of time, and by so many authors, that reveals such remarkable uniformity of conclusions and validations.

A good example is the phenomenal spiritual link of the Genesis Creation, the story of God's Covenant People, all the way to the Cross of Jesus and the Gospel of Grace, to the seventh day Sabbath.

At the end of the Creation week, on the seventh day, God sanctified and rested on Sabbath. In the Gospels, we read that Jesus, the Son of God and Messiah, at the end of His life, after that afternoon when he died on the Cross, was buried and then rested in the grave on the seventh day Sabbath.

At the end of the Gospels, the Lord Jesus reveals the vital global task of sharing His life, crucifixion, resurrection and teachings with the then known world. He wanted to prepare God's people to take His gospel of joy and salvation to the whole world. God had previously tried all kinds of ways to get through to mankind. Starting in the beautiful Garden of Eden, and then the flood, the Israelite bondage in Egypt, Sinai, the preaching of the prophets, and now – CALVARY.

Matthew 28:18-20: "Jesus came near and spoke to the Disciples, "I've received all authority in heaven and on earth. Therefore, go and make disciples of all nations, baptizing them in the name of the Father and of the Son and of the Holy Spirit, teaching them to obey everything that I've commanded you. Look, I myself will be with you every day until the end of this present age."

By the end of the Gospels, the disciples were feeling inadequate to continue the task that the Lord Jesus gave them. They were filled with tremendous anxiety and awe for the life changing task of sharing Jesus' Gospel. After the ascension of Jesus chronicled in the next chapter of the New Testament (Acts 1), they waited for the promised fulfillment and empowerment to prepare them for the task. Little did they know of the wonder and power that they were soon to experience.

Acts 2:1-6 the Day of Pentecost - "When the day of Pentecost arrived, they were all together in one place. Suddenly a sound from heaven like the howling of a fierce wind filled the entire house where they were sitting. They saw what seemed to be individual flames of fire alighting on each one of them. They were all filled with the Holy Spirit and began to speak in other languages as the Spirit enabled them to speak.

There were pious Jews from every nation under heaven living in Jerusalem. When they heard this sound, a crowd gathered. They were mystified because everyone heard them speaking in their native languages."

This is a well-known historic narrative, but there are some events in Acts chapter 2 that are often lost or missed out, which are essential in understanding the early formation of the Christian Church. These include the real meaning of the Day of Pentecost, and the new experience of tongues. In reading the King James Version the use of *'tongues'* is understood by most commentaries as the miraculous ability to speak in real, foreign languages.

Firstly, the Day of Pentecost is universally remembered as the day that the Holy Spirit was poured out enabling God's people to share the Gospel of Jesus, the Cross and Redemption. The little-known fact is that the Day of Pentecost, fifty days after Passover, was in fact the Old Testament feast-day to commemorate the giving of the Ten Commandments on Sinai.

We also need to remember the prophetic and liturgical history of God's chosen people. The Day of Pentecost was not part of the Passover and other festivals that were prophetic festivals of the coming of the Messiah.

Pentecost or Shavuot has many names in the Bible (the Feast of Weeks, the Feast of Harvest, and the Latter Firstfruits). Celebrated on the fiftieth day after Passover, Shavuot is traditionally a joyous time of giving thanks and presenting offerings for the new grain of the summer wheat harvest in Israel. The name "Feast of Weeks" was given because God commanded the Jews in Leviticus 23:15-16, to count seven full weeks (or 49 days) beginning on the second day of Passover, and then present offerings of new grain to the Lord as a lasting ordinance.

Shavuot was originally a festival for expressing thankfulness to the Lord for the blessing of the harvest. And because it occurred after the Passover, it acquired the name "Latter Firstfruits." The celebration is also tied to the giving of the Ten Commandments and thus bears the name *Matin Torah* or "giving of the Law."

Jews believe that it was exactly at this time that God gave the Torah to the people through Moses on Mount Sinai. This is significant for us to remember, because when the Disciples were gathered early in the history of the new Christian Church as we read in the book of Acts, they were honoring the giving of the Ten Commandments. In John 14:15 Jesus says "If you love me, keep my commandments."

One lesson is that the young Christian church was firmly built on the Ten Commandments, and that it was not only for the Jews, but also for Gentile converts to the new Christian Way. In Romans chapter 3 Paul specifically brings to light a discussion of the difference between Jew and Gentile in the new Christianity, and writes in Romans 3:31 "Do we then cancel the Law through this faith? Absolutely not! Instead, we confirm the Law."

Secondly, in the discussion and report of Acts chapter 2, we find that there were people present from at least sixteen different language groups, from Parthians to Arabs. When the Apostles spoke using their own language, the crowds of people each heard the message in their own language. This means that the gift was not speaking in foreign languages or a gift of tongues, but rather a gift of ears, because these 16 language groups each heard it in their own language.

Thirdly, in validating the importance of this Day of Pentecost, the miraculous events, and the inspiration of the Holy Spirit, we must not forget the verities that were taught on this day. Acts 2:23, 24; 31-33 "In accordance with God's established plan and foresight, he was betrayed. You, with the help of wicked men, had Jesus killed by nailing him to a cross. God raised him up! God freed him from death's dreadful grip, since it was impossible for death to hang on to him. Having seen this beforehand, David spoke about the resurrection of Christ, and that he wasn't abandoned to the grave, nor did his body experience decay. This Jesus, God raised up. We are all witnesses to that fact. He was exalted to God's right side and received from the Father the promised Holy Spirit. He poured out this Spirit, and you are seeing and hearing the results of his having done so."

2 Timothy 4:3, 4 "There will come a time when people will not tolerate sound teaching. They will collect teachers who say what they want to hear because they are self-centered. They will turn their back on the truth and turn to myths. But you must keep control of yourself in all circumstances."

Commenting on this verse, Matthew Henry writes "People will turn away from the truth, they will grow weary of the plain gospel of Christ, they will be greedy of fables, and take pleasure in them. People do so when they will not endure that preaching which is searching, plain, and to the purpose. Those who love souls must be ever watchful, must venture and bear all the painful effects of their faithfulness, and take all opportunities of making known the pure gospel."

The challenge we have in our contemporary church is: are we going to follow the way of the world, of Babylon, of fallen churches, of Laodicea, and of itching ears?

To many minds in our modern world the events and miracles of the Son of God and the Holy Spirit are not easy to comprehend and believe. It is almost beyond the scope of our minds, but when the facts about Jesus' Crucifixion touches our hearts, or the center of our lives, we experience changes, healing and miracles that we did not even dream of before. This is what the Cross does to us. A cruel instrument of Roman torture and death became a symbol of grace, mercy, hope and love.

Ephesians 2:8 and 9
"For by grace you have been saved through faith,
And that not of yourselves; it is the gift of God,
Not of works, lest anyone should boast.

Christian missionaries and evangelists have reached the farthest outposts of civilization since Apostolic times, fulfilling the command of Matthew 28:19, 20 "Go therefore and make disciples of all the nations, baptizing them in the name of the Father and of the Son and of the Holy Spirit, teaching them to observe all things that I have commanded you; and lo, I am with you always, *even* to the end of the age." Thousands of brave dedicated men and women travelled thousands of miles and labored many years caring for the medical, educational, spiritual and social lives of peoples and tribes on all continents and islands.

Now as most of the planet has been exposed to the grace, love and lifestyles of Christianity, where are we standing?

Have we fulfilled our mission?

Are we ready, and have the global population ready, for the end of time?

More than 1,400 years ago, the Islamic armies of Mohammed, the Caliphs and other Muslim forces conquered nations all the way into Western Europe. In the 7th century, Muslim armies conquered most of Spain, calling it Al-Andulus. They would not be completely expelled for 700 years, the year Columbus discovered the new world.

These days Muslims are returning, and polls suggest they are not returning to be Spaniards or Europeans. The original invasion of Islamic army centuries ago consisted of tens of thousands of well-trained invaders attacking with swords, cutting people's heads off.

Today the alarming statistic is that more than 60 million Muslims have invaded Christian, Western and Free Market countries with air tickets and illegal crossings since the Second World War! This number includes more than 10 million in the United States of America.

These illegal immigrants and refugees are bringing in millions more. These people are not armed with swords, but with the power of mass mobs. Their motives are the same, Jihad! The goal is to set up global Caliphates and prepare the whole world for the coming the Mahdi or Muslim Messiah. We need to remember that all of Islam, Muslims, ISIS, ISIL, is primarily and fundamentally a greedy, power hungry and bloodthirsty political power seeking world domination.

Meanwhile western nations are crumbling within. When will the military, social, and economic collapse happen?

Just open your eyes and take a look around the world. The next wave of the implosion of money may not have reached Wall Street yet, but it is deeply affecting billions of lives all over the planet. On our Earth, at least 80% of the global population lives on less than $10 a day. Over three billion people live on less than $2.50 a day. More than 80% live in countries where income disparity is increasing. According to UNICEF 22,000 impoverished children die every day. They die quietly in some of the poorest villages on earth, far removed from the scrutiny and the conscience of the world. Being meek and weak in life makes these dying multitudes even more invisible in death.

Problems of healthcare, buying food, financing a home and car, and even paying for basics such as clothing and education, are growing like creeping leprosy amongst the middle classes. Have you heard of the boomerang kids? Young people returning to their parental homes after college, after divorce, after not being able to get jobs. Here are some facts that we find in America:

- **Fact:** College tuition is up 600% plus since 2001.
- **Fact:** 85 % of college graduates go back to live with their parents. These are the *boomerang kids* who keep going back home.
- **Fact:** Student loans total more than one trillion dollars.
- **Fact:** The average graduate student starts out with $25,000 in debt.
- **Fact:** If you marry another graduate student, you start out your marriage with at least $50,000 in debt.

Other increasing dilemmas that many societies face today are a lack of food and water, religious fanaticism, political corruption and greed, failing energy sources, inequality, poverty and global financial collapse. According to my Bible, these are all signs that this tired old Earth is heading to a devastating end.

Where can we find answers and solutions that no scientist, social engineer, politician or philosopher can find? It seems that the more PhD's in Economy and MBA's in Business Management we have, the worse our economy, finances and lifestyles are getting. It seems that the more marriage and relationship counselors we have, the more anger, fighting, divorce, dysfunctional families and relationship break-ups society is facing. The more sophisticated some areas of the world become, the greater distress and hunger develop in other areas.

Infectious diseases continue to blight the lives of the poor across the world. An estimated 40 million people are living with HIV/AIDS, with 3 million deaths each year. Every year there are 350–500 million cases of malaria, with 1 million fatalities. Africa accounts for 90 percent of malarial deaths and African children account for over 80 percent of malaria victims worldwide. Now there are new diseases such as rapidly developing strains of sexually transmitted diseases that have no antidote. By the time they have the symptoms, there is nothing the patient can do.

Where do we go to understand the inequality, unfairness and instability of this world? In the sophisticated capitalist nations, we have top heavy management and a shortage of unskilled labor. The other day I visited a medical center in the USA to find tht there were more cars parked in the employee parking lot, than the total number of patient beds in the hospital. For every American soldier enduring the intensity of the front lines, there are at least 22 military employees backing him up in some office or staring at computers.

The outcomes in education, economy and safety, peace keeping, health care and just getting through another day are all devolving instead of evolving. The gap between the *haves* and the *have-nots* is widening.

Social groups and institutions are not just experiencing burnout, but are slowly fizzling out.

Add to this the Laodicean condition of the modern Christian Church. Revelation 3:15 "I know your works, that you are neither cold nor hot." Are God's people in these times living in Jesus' Covenant of Grace, or just limping along? This lukewarm condition is rampant all over the world. We now have a world full of scientists who have no faith and the faithful who have no rationality, and this is not good for God's Church at the end of time.

Are there any answers in the Word of God?

Does God really care for us?

Does the Bible give us the way out?

Does the Bible have a plan for us?

The following pages have grown out of a sincere and intensive Scriptural search and study of God's Word and Covenants. It is not based on systematic theology, which involves the applications, perceptions, exegesis and opinions of Biblical scholars, authors and theologians.

The primary source for these pages is mostly from Biblical Theology. The focal source is the Word of God and information used comes from studying different Bible translations and original texts. Many of the ideas, even though Biblical, are presented in a unique way and not intended as a theological enterprise, but rather as a homiletic and spiritual sharing of the Gospel of God's wonderful grace.

The purpose is that this will be a gospel and an evangelistic tool to share with persons looking for a closer walk with Jesus as Creator and Redeemer, Jesus as Lord of Lords and King of Kings.

The invitation for everyone is to become a part of God's Covenant People, His Remnant and those saved by the Blood of the Lamb. Since Calvary 2,000 years ago, our redemption is not from being a member of a 'chosen' race or group, but is personal and a direct individual relationship with God the Father, Jesus Christ, and the Holy Spirit.

Many mistakes have been made by Christian Bible expositors using wrong methods, methodologies and world views. The following is an example.

The teaching of the old versus new covenant is the result of dispensational dogma and puts a spin on what God is really telling us through the prophets.

There is a remarkable prophecy in Jeremiah 31:31-34, "Behold, the days are coming, says the LORD, when I will make a new covenant with the house of Israel and with the house of Judah - according to the covenant that I made with their fathers in the day that I took them by the hand to lead them out of the land of Egypt, My covenant which they broke, though I was a husband to them, says the LORD. But this is the covenant that I will make with the house of Israel after those days, says the LORD: I will put My law in their minds, and write it on their hearts; and I will be their God, and they shall be My people. No more shall every man teach his neighbor, and every man his brother, saying, 'Know the LORD,' for they all shall know Me, from the least of them to the greatest of them, says the LORD. For I will forgive their iniquity, and their sin I will remember no more."

What we comprehend here, is that the Son of God, Jesus, played a significant part in Creation as well as Redemption. His amazing grace weaves through the Scriptures from Genesis to Revelation. There are some very clear Bible proofs that the Lord Jesus created the Earth and all on it. John 1:1, "He was in the world, and the world was made through Him." Hebrews 1:10 "You, LORD, in the beginning laid the foundation of the earth, and the heavens are the work of Your hands." This text in the book of Hebrews proclaim Jesus Christ as Creator, and also as LORD." Whenever the word LORD (*Kurios* in Greek and *JHWH* in Hebrew) appears in capital letters in English Bibles, it refers the Divinity and Lordship of our Savior Jesus Christ.

Some dispensationalists say that the Old Testament is based on *works* and the New Testament on *grace*, but the truth is that the Old Testament often mentions grace.

The teachings of God's grace permeate the entire Bible, right from the beginning in Genesis 6:8, "But Noah found grace in the eyes of the LORD" to Psalm, 84:10, 11 "For a day in Your courts is better than a thousand. I would rather be a doorkeeper in the house of my God than dwell in the tents of wickedness. For the LORD God is a sun and shield; The LORD will give grace and glory; no good thing will He withhold from those who walk uprightly." Near the end of the Old Testament, the prophet proclaims in Zechariah 12:10 "And I will pour on the house of David and on the inhabitants of Jerusalem the Spirit of grace and supplication; then they will look on Me whom they pierced." The Bible ends with the words of Revelation 22:21 "The grace of our Lord Jesus Christ be with you all."

There is no doubt that the wonderful grace of God became better understood and experienced after the life, ministry and death of His only son Jesus on a cruel Roman cross. The fact is that it was always there. Available to Noah, Abraham, Isaac, Jacob, Moses, King David and all the kings, patriarchs and prophets. This same grace is now extended to non-Jews, to the Gentiles (other nations), as the early Christian church taught Acts 15:11 "And I will pour on the house of David and on the inhabitants of Jerusalem (*Gentiles*) the Spirit of grace and supplication; then they will look on Me whom they pierced." The apostle Paul reminds us of the source of his conversion and spiritual strength in 2 Corinthians 12:9 "My (*Jesus'*) grace is sufficient for you, for My strength is made perfect in weakness."

There are some factual truths that we can learn from the context of the Cross of Calvary and Jesus' sacrificial death for us. There was a chain of miraculous events that give tremendous validity to the uniqueness of Jesus Christ and His claims that he is the Son of God. As a result, we find that redemption comes through faith in Him only. These facts together shape an unbreakable chain of evidence that authenticates and declares Jesus Christ as truly the Son of God and the redemptive Savior of the mankind.

The Cross is the key that unlocks our hearts and lives to new spirituality and new lifestyles in Jesus.

C. H. Spurgeon preached a sermon at the Music Hall in Royal Surrey Gardens on September 4, 1859, with the title

'*The Blood of the Everlasting Covenant.*' He read from Hebrews 13:20 "Now may the God of peace who brought up our Lord Jesus from the dead, that great Shepherd of the sheep, through the blood of the everlasting covenant, make you complete..." and went on to say "It is called an everlasting covenant. And here you observe at once its *antiquity*. The covenant of grace is the oldest of all things. It is sometimes a subject of great joy to me to think that the covenant of grace is older than the covenant of works. The covenant of works had a beginning, but the covenant of grace had not; and blessed be God the covenant of works has its end, but the covenant of grace shall stand fast when heaven and earth shall pass away."

Jesus our Messiah died on the cruel Cross of Calvary for all. For all sinners. Before Calvary in Old Testament times. After Calvary in New Testament times. Now for all living this side of the Cross and into the 21st Century Anno Domini.

But now the Cross is empty.

The tomb is empty.

Jesus is our High Priest in the Heavenly Sanctuary.

Jesus is Lord and Savior.

He is coming soon.

Spirituality

Is there a 'God gene' built into each person?

Is God inside or outside us?

What is spirituality?

Many people say that they are spiritual. Some say they are not religious, but they are spiritual. Some eastern religions exercise their spirituality by meditating inwardly, and 'emptying self.'

On the other hand, most of Christianity finds its spirituality by praying to God outside of themselves, in Heaven and omnipresent. The Bible teaches that humans are created in the image of God (Genesis 1:27) and the invitation of the Gospel of Jesus is to have this image restored. The entire brain, body, all our behavior, feelings, and thoughts, are dedicated to God. "And whatever you do in word or deed, do all in the name of the Lord Jesus, giving thanks to God the Father through Him" Colossians 3:17.

There are three main elements for meaningful Christian growth, vitality and lifestyle. These are justification, sanctification and glorification. Romans 3:23, 24 "For all have sinned and fall short of the glory of God, being justified freely by His grace through the redemption that is in Christ Jesus." To be justified means to be forgiven. It depends on the sinner's desire to be justified, to have complete confidence in Jesus Christ and the efficacy of the Blood of the Lamb to wipe away all sin.

Sanctification means to be set aside, to be made holy, and only God can do this. There are no dead saints. Only living saints! A living, vibrant Christian lifestyle includes coming to Jesus daily, living by the power of the Holy Spirit, and enjoying the best life that God has for you each day.

The final step is glorification. Jesus is coming again to take us home. Our Lord says in John 14:1-3 "Let not your heart be troubled; you believe in God, believe also in Me. In My Father's house are many mansions; if it were not so, I would have told you. I go to prepare a place for you. And if I go and prepare a place for you, I will come again and receive you to Myself; that where I am, there you may be also."

Psalms 139:13-15

"You made all the delicate, inner parts of my body
and knit me together in my mother's womb.
Thank you for making me so wonderfully complex!
Your workmanship is marvelous-and how well I know it.
You watched me as I was being formed in utter seclusion
You know me inside and out,
You know every bone in my body;
You know exactly how I was made, bit by bit,
how I was sculpted from nothing into something.
As I was woven together in the dark of the parts of the Earth."

The Good News of the Word of God is not how good and how great people are, but how gracious and merciful God is, in spite of our sin, rebellion and depravity.

Humanity needs much more than a role model.

We need a Savior.

The man Jesus came from ordinary people because He came for all people.

Christianity isn't just for the pure, the talented, the good, the humble and the honest. The story of Jesus Christ was written to change lives of the impure, sinners, calculating schemers, the proud, the dishonest, and by those without meaning in life. Nobody is so bad, so insignificant, so devoid of talent, or so outside the circle of faith, that he or she is outside the story of Christ. Nobody on Earth is so perfect and wonderful that they do not need Jesus.

A word that is used wrong 99% of the time, is the word *spirituality*. It is often used as being a part of the human person or mindset, usually as an attribute that denotes a frame of mind or sensitivity to religious values. The word spirituality has been used in wrong contexts over many centuries. Even great minds, authors, philosophers, psychologists and students erroneously imply that the components of the human personality consist of 'mind, body and spirit' or 'mind, body and soul.' These are false trichotomies and contrasts. We need much more prayer, deep rational thinking and revision. The term *spirituality* is often used glibly or lightly with a meaning of holiness or mysticism. The fact is that scientists and researchers have not found any part of our brain that is *spiritual*.

Real Christian spirituality is an individual's personal relationship with God, based on religion, beliefs and values.

It includes our acts, beliefs and faith. What does it mean when we talk about mind, body and soul?

- The word *mind* simply refers to our brain, thought, cognitions and memory.
- *Body* refers to our physical being, behavior and anatomical nature.
- The word *soul* does not need a lot of explanation, except that it is a synonym or alternative for the word *life*. A person does not **have** a soul, he or she **is a living soul**.

What is logical and clear is that our personalities consist of three main areas: feelings, cognitions and behavior. This is found in our whole brain and neurological system. Depending on DNA and early socialization, the experience, extent and intensity of these three areas is differs. Recent research shows that most of our attitudes, ways we do things, the food we like or hate and many other traits are established during the toddler years of 1 to 2 years old.

Habit or temperament formation is the process by which newly learned behaviors become automatic. If you instinctively reach for coffee the moment you wake up in the morning, you have a habit. By the same token, if you feel inclined to lace up your running shoes and hit the streets as soon as you get home, you have acquired a habit. Old habits are hard to break and new habits are hard to form. That is because the behavioral patterns we repeat most often are literally etched into our neural pathways. The good news is that, through repetition, it is possible to form new habits and maintain them.

The fundamental components of personality are:

- Mind – soul, presence of mind, clarity, conscience, understanding and memory
- Body and physical vitality - perseverance and endurance for work and behavior
- Feelings, emotions, warmth and empathy, sadness, happiness and anger

It is easy to state the above, but not so simple to classify individuals' personalities and temperament. Some people are more feeling, including 'happy clappies' and other emotional groups. Some folks are more thinking or rational, for example theologians and denominations with gnostic beliefs. Some are more doing, acting or behavioral. Each individual has wide ranging differences, broader or narrower individualities that make up their total persona.

This also applies to the followers of Jesus Christ. This is how God made us different and how we grow up with differences and changing world views. The fact is that you can play a part in your own growth, socialization or re-socialization.

You can change.

Learning, behavior, experience, trauma, being 'born again,' and intense therapy and other events can change us.

You may ask "where then is my spirituality?"

It consists in each of the three aspects of our personality: thinking, feeling and behavior. This differs in extent and ratio from person to person. You may be more right brained, left brained, or dependent on your frontal lobe where morals and conscience are found.

If there was a spirituality meter it would show that your lifestyle is different to other persons. Some are more doing (religious), or more feeling (happy or sad), and some are more thinking or philosophical (rational). This is the reason why there are so many personalities, religions and churches. This is the reason why Jesus had four Gospels, twelve Disciples, and related different parables that would affect diverse people in different ways.

Most of us are somewhere within the range of these three aspects of our lives. We are all different, and this is the reason why committees with many differing viewpoints are good for reaching decisions, and also why Jesus in His ministry talked with a variety of persons, so that there is something that will touch each heart. This wide difference in temperament is also a source of conflict, but this needs to be understood and lead to understanding, acceptance, and conciliation.

1 Corinthians 12:4-11 "There are different spiritual gifts but the same Spirit; and there are different ministries and the same Lord; and there are different activities but the same God who produces all of them in everyone. A demonstration of the Spirit is given to each person for the common good. A word of wisdom is given by the Spirit to one person, a word of knowledge to another (*a thinking person*) according to the same Spirit, faith to still another by the same Spirit, gifts of healing to another in the one Spirit, performance of miracles (*behavior*) to another, prophecy to another, the ability to tell spirits apart to another, different kinds of tongues to another, and the interpretation of the tongues to another. All these things are produced by the one and same Spirit who gives what he wants to each person."

Spirituality is not an opinion about God, but a walk with God. It is a journey with Jesus Christ rather than a journey to Christ. Spirituality is a conscious personal response to the love and grace of God, a daily and life-long relationship, and a healthy balanced journey in the Word of God. It is exercised through the faith, feelings and actions of each individual. A spiritual lifestyle includes worshipping God the Father, being rooted in Jesus Christ, and empowered by the Holy Spirit. This does not mean that you have to separate yourself from the world, but that your life is authentic, meaningful and useful to the world you are living in. It does not mean that you are free of sickness, despair, grief and problems, but that you can still enjoy grace and peace through all of this. In this life it does not promise the absence of disease, disorder and distress, but does offer healing, hope and heaven.

In the Bible there are many instances of emotions or feelings. These include hate (Cain); anger (Moses); happiness (those healed or saved by Jesus); and behavior or works (Revelation 2:2 "I know your works, your labor, and your endurance.") Our Creator God loves us all. God only wants the best for you, and that includes living a balanced healthy life, and wants you to live to the best of your abilities that have been endowed to you. With the plan of salvation that God has prepared for those who follow Him, there is light at the end of the tunnel.

Some folks say "I'm so busy - I just don't have enough time to complete all my work." Do you need a break, but doubt you have time for it? What about those who do not have sufficient work to sustain themselves? The practice of appreciating the Sabbath helps us to resist the tyranny of too much or too little work. We not only honor the Sabbath, but we develop a good work ethic of working six days each week. If you work a four or five-day week, then you have time to do more work at home.

Spirituality is not an opinion about God, but a walk with God. It is a journey with Jesus Christ, rather than a journey to Christ. Spirituality is a conscious personal response to the love and grace of God, a daily and life-long relationship, and a healthy balanced journey in the Word of God. It is exercised through the faith, feelings and actions of each individual.

There are some people who postulate that religion and spirituality are two different perceptions, but analyzing and comparing the two, religion and spirituality, is a false dichotomy. They belong together.

We all need both religion and spirituality. Religion is the doing part of our faith, and spirituality is our personal walk and relationship with God. Whichever way we define this relationship, in Christianity our spiritualty is built on our religious beliefs, values and structures. Our spirituality is built on the Rock Jesus Christ and His amazing grace.

There is a paucity in understanding the concept of religion, when some declare that even secular humanism is a religion. Christians need to stand up and say that religion is not secular or mere abandonment. Sociologists have for more than a hundred years stated that a religion has at least three facets: the worship of a Supreme Being; a system of rules or regulations; and the sharing of beliefs. This means that you really cannot be a free flowing 'spiritual' person.

Real spirituality includes religious belief and practice. All the holy men sitting in their earth colored blankets, begging for food and money, that I saw in India, are in reality not humble, kind or spiritual. They are narcissistic.

Spirituality is an important part of the Sabbath. The word 'spirituality' has been misused and abused so much by all kinds of pseudo and quasi religions, to the extent that it is less used in Protestant churches. As members of Jesus' body, His church, we need to reclaim the authentic experience of spiritual enjoyment and perceptions.

Christian spirituality is an individual's personal inward relationship with God. This includes the affect (feelings or emotions), the behavioral, and the cognitive, (our acts and thinking) facets of our lives. Our differing spiritual experience depends on how much of each of these three aspects is utilized in our lives and lifestyles.

Ask yourself, am I more of a feeler, a doer or a thinker?

Spirituality is mostly formed during childhood development. A person sometimes needs to go all the way back and talk about these formative years in order to understand spiritual feelings and beliefs or the lack of them. For example, research has shown that people who attend church and lead lives that include goal-directed spiritual disciplines, are healthier and live on average longer than persons who do not. This is just one of the positive benefits of being a child of God.

There needs to be room for God in each person's heart and life. Our God and Creator calls all at some time in your life to have faith, real living practical faith in Him. Christians believe in the Godhead or Trinity. Different factors and symbols can be used to describe the three distinct persons in the Godhead and to illustrate the fact that they are one.

A few years ago, I stood on the southernmost tip of India at the fishing village of Kanyakumari. I stepped down the rocky stairs into the water where three oceans meet, the Indian Ocean, the Arabian Sea, and the Bay of Bengal. Three oceans, but really one. God is like that, but even more. Another symbol used to describe God is an apple with its peel, flesh, and seeds. Each is distinct, but they form one apple. Each member of the Godhead, the Father, Son, and Holy Spirit, is distinct but they are still one.

There are always problems when we make the Christian religion too argumentative and apologetic. The Christian faith as well as the Bible have an inspiring perspective of proclamation and redemption, and not of looking for excuses or reasons to condemn other persons. Primary spiritual experience is at its core, and not the philosophy and psychology of the times.

In the early days of Christianity, the Church used Greek and Roman thought to help amplify and illustrate the essential experience of faith. What was clear then and is now, is that the focus was on the experience of God's grace and our faith, and not in the use of rational explanations to get people to feel bad about themselves. To the early Christians experience was primary and understanding was secondary. Knowledge was experiential and not just a cranial activity or feeling.

Faith is also an important component of the seventh day Sabbath. Faith is not just a state of believing, but a state of trusting in the Source that makes faith possible. Therefore, when it comes to spirituality, your faith is not just in your theological or dogmatic beliefs, but rather in God who acts in reconciling the world to Him, and bridging the gap that sin and rebellion has caused between God and humans. The Bible repeats over and over again that both faith and obedience are needed.

Ephesians 2:8 "For by grace you have been saved through faith, and that not of yourselves; it is the gift of God."

There are many benefits to enjoying spiritual health. Research has shown that spiritual well-being has a significant negative correlation with loneliness, and that loneliness has a high correlation with cardiac disease. That is why a person who is spiritually well has greater trust in life, experiences hope and feelings of being loved, and also has a smaller chance of developing heart disease. The ability to deal with chronic pain is also made easier by enjoying spiritual well-being. On the other hand, spiritual distress can increase the incidence of depression, and lowers resistance to disease by weakening the immune system.

During the Iraq war, panic and fear of terrorist attacks, sales of duct tape and plastic sheeting increased tremendously, especially in the United States. We have been living under an emergency, according to Biblical dating, for more than six thousand years. Many hurt and scared Christians have found that duct tape, glue, gas masks, emergency supplies and escape routes do not really help. The healing, safety, peace, and assurance that we need are all in Jesus and in practical daily Christian living through the leading and power of the Holy Spirit. This includes:

Healing in Jesus
Safety in Jesus

Peace because of Jesus

Assurance through Jesus

Another important element of Christian belief is love. You may ask, what is *love*? Millions have asked of the spiritual experience 'is it a feeling?' or 'is it an intellectual exercise?' or 'is it doing something for the person you love?' The fact is that all forms of genuine 'love' include each of these three aspects of our personality and being. Real 'love' is feeling good, trusting, doing things together, and pleasant thoughts. It is also going through disappointments and struggles together. These are always helpful and practical. Love is existential and the extent cannot always be calculated by analyzing the framework and domains of feelings, thoughts and actions. If you love someone, you do not mind washing the dishes or cleaning the car.

Love is an important dimension of God's plan for our spiritual lives and the Sabbath of God. I like to call my Bible a love letter from God. There is just so much, so many stories, so much victory that we need to have the freeing experience that the word of God proclaims, and shares new messages of encouragement each day.

Paul sends the same message to the fledgling church in Colossae. Colossians 1:25-27 "I became a minister according by the commission God gave to me, to present the word of God, the mystery which has been hidden from ages and from generations, but now has been revealed to His saints. To them God willed to make known what are the riches of the glory of this mystery among the Gentiles: which is Christ in you, the hope of glory." This secret or mystery that God prepared was His Only Son dying on the cruel Roman cross to set you free.

A missionary in Zambia once shared a pertinent experience with a practical moral lesson. Once a month he used the mission truck to go to the city to buy supplies. During one trip, apart from food, books, medical and building supplies, he bought some plants, trees and shrubs for the campus garden. Back at the mission, he gave these to the gardener to plant. He showed the man where to plant them to make the campus look more beautiful.

They watered and watched the trees and shrubs carefully for the next year, but they did not seem to grow much. The lack of growth worried him, and after the next year, he asked the gardener to dig around the plants to see what was wrong. It shocked him to find that the gardener had left the trees and shrubs in the original nursery pots or containers, resulting in the roots being stunted and not growing or spreading for water and nutrition! He then asked the gardener to dig all the plants out, remove the containers, replant, fertilize, and water them. Zambia is a fertile land with good rainfall and the plants grew like never before!

Our lives are often just like that. Our roots got stuck in the deceptions and fabrications of the past. We are stunted, reserved, restrained, repressed and we hold back, but from the time we let go and let God, there is no limit to our healing, growth and spiritual maturity. From the time we let God through the power of the Holy Spirit and the blood of Jesus remove the obstacles that are inhibiting our emotional, mental, and physical growth and maturity, we enjoy new life, vibrant spirituality, and better relationships.

The awesome truth is that our Lord has made it all possible for us. His marvelous and amazing grace preceded our lives. God put in place a plan way back in the Garden of

Eden when our first parents sinned, and then affirmed it 2,000 years ago on a hill called Calvary, when His only Son died on a cruel cross for our deliverance. This healing of the blood of Jesus our Savior is here right now, waiting for our faith, trust and acceptance. Despite our brokenness, God calls each person and makes it possible for us to choose to follow a just and merciful God.

The earthly ministry of our Lord Jesus reveals that His spiritual journey included a wholistic (whole) and holistic (holy) approach whereby He reached out to the emotional, mental and physical needs of people. He healed the sick, gave the hungry crowds food, and helped them to feel better. He then taught them with the use of Scripture and stories of the day. He loved children. Jesus also revealed His spirituality by obeying what His Father expected of Him. He said: "If you love me, keep my commandments" John 14:15. Through His words and acts, His empathy and kindness, His truth and testimony, His love and grace, Jesus modeled and set a balanced example of the Christian spiritual lifestyle. Romans 2:15 "They show the work of the law written in their hearts, their conscience also bearing witness, and between themselves their thoughts accusing or else excusing them."

Being a free moral agent is a significant part of your spiritual personality. Our concept of freedom not only affects our way of thinking about ourselves, but also our relationships with other persons. When you allow yourself freedom, you will allow others their freedom. When you have the freedom to consider alternate choices for yourself, you will let other people decide for themselves.

9

Paul's Letters to 7 Churches

*"A person should think about us this way - as servants
of Christ and managers of God's secrets."*
1 Corinthians 4:1

Paul's Deep Spiritual Experience - The Apostle Paul
records his intense and profound religious and spiritual
journey in letters to seven churches in the New Testament.
These were to the Christians in Rome, Corinth, Galatia,
Ephesus, Philippi, Colossae and Thessalonica.

The challenges that Paul encountered in the early
Christian church were much the same as we still find
prevalent today. The Christian church is infiltrated with

normal men and women, and unfortunately normal results personality clashes and disputes in groups.

An example of creeping untruths and the assimilation of false, often Pagan, often Judaizing, are the events of the third century after the establishing of the church with Paul and James as the early leaders, and the effects of pagan and heathen teachings.

Emperor Constantine: The reign of Constantine can to be interpreted against the background of his personal ambiguity. Roman opinion expected of its emperors not innovation but the preservation of traditional ways. Ancient Rome's propaganda and political covetousness were conditioned, by declaration, allusion, and symbols, to express these goals. An example of this was that pagan gods and their symbols have survived for many centuries.

When you visit the city of Rome, the piazzas, churches, ancient ruins, and especially Saint Peter's square, you see many statues and examples of Paganism that have survived, but had names and titles changed to Christian names.

Pagan idols became Christian idols. From the time of Emperor Constantine, paganism sneaked in to the Christian church. It is important to remember that Constantine was a pagan and a henotheist.

Henotheism is the belief that many gods exist, but the worship of only one of these gods is selected. A henotheist accepts that many gods exist and can be worshipped. However, the henotheist chooses to mainly worship one of these gods. Henotheism is the belief in one god without denying the existence of others.

Hindus that I saw in India are a good example of this belief in practice. Hindus generally worship one god, yet acknowledge that there are many other gods, often millions, that can be worshiped as well. The religion of the ancient Greeks and their worship of the Olympians is another well-known example, with Zeus being the supreme ruler of eleven other gods.

Constantine the Great was born in England during the decade of 280 AD, growing up in a family that worshipped pagan idols. He later followed his father into battles and experienced the thrill of many victories.

He eventually rose to the position of Emperor of the Pagan Roman Empire. His greatest greed and motivation was that the Roman Empire should rule the whole world, all peoples, and all religions. We visited the triumphal arch in Rome that was built and dedicated to his honor and victory over Maxentious. The inscription reads 'This Victory Was Due to the Power of the Divine Constantine of the Senate of Rome.'

In the dedication of the city of Constantinople in 330 AD, the ceremonies were half pagan, half Christian. The chariot of the sun-god was set in the market-place, and over its head was placed the Cross of Christ, while the *Kyrie Eleison* (the Lord have mercy upon us) was sung. Shortly before his death, Constantine confirmed the privileges of the priests of the ancient gods. Many other actions of his have also the appearance of half-measures, as if he himself had wavered and had always held to some form of syncretistic religion. The believers in Mithras observed Sunday as well as Christmas. Consequently, Constantine speaks not of the day of the Lord, but of the everlasting day of the sun.

Constantine's complete name is Flavius Valerius Aurelius Constantinus Augustus. He is also known as Constantine I or Saint Constantine. He was a solar henotheist, meaning he believed that the Roman sun god, *Sol*, was the visible manifestation of an invisible 'Highest God' (*summus deus*), who was the principle behind the universe.

In AD 312 Constantine invaded Italy. Constantine later claimed to have had a vision on the way to Rome, during the night before battle. In this dream, he supposedly saw the '*Chi-Ro*', the symbol of Christ, shining above the sun. Seeing this as a divine sign, it is said that Constantine had his soldiers paint the symbol on their shields. These days symbols of the sun and cross are found in the Catholic Eucharist.

Following this, Constantine went on to defeat the numerically stronger army of Maxentius at the Battle at the Milvian Bridge (October 312 AD). Constantine's opponent Maxentius, together with thousands of his soldiers, drowned as the bridge of boats his force was retreating over collapsed.

Constantine saw this victory as directly related to the vision he had had the night before. From then on Constantine saw himself as an 'emperor of the Christian people'. Whether this made him a Christian is the subject of debate, but Constantine, who only had himself baptized on his deathbed, is generally understood as the first Christian emperor of the Roman world. Despite this turn toward Christianity, Constantine remained very tolerant of the old pagan religions. His worship of the sun god was still important to him and his Pagan followers. This can be seen on the carvings of his triumphal Arch in Rome and on coins minted during his reign.

Constantine eventually became sole emperor of the entire Roman world. His reign was that of a hard, utterly determined and ruthless man. In the spring of 337 AD, Constantine fell ill. Realizing that he was about to die, he asked to be baptized. This was performed on his deathbed by Eusebius, bishop of Nicomedia. Constantine died on 22 May, 337 AD in the imperial villa at Ankyrona. His body was carried to the Church of the Holy Apostles, his mausoleum. A bizarre decision elevated him, the first Christian emperor, to the status of an old pagan god.

The acceptance of Constantine's *Day of the Sun* by Papal decree, opened the way to call Sunday the Day of the Lord. Therefore, this is not a Biblical Christian day of worship. It is rather an appeasement by the Roman Church to bring the Pagan worship of the Sun and the Cross of Jesus together.

What does the Word of God teach?

We can all learn something from the Apostle Paul's dogmatic stance in his letters. There were errors creeping into the young church. In fact, the whole Word of God shows us the power and results of choices we make, such as, you can choose to be like Cain or Abel, Abraham or Lot, David or Saul, or maybe Peter or Judas. God gives you the choice about where you would like to spend eternity - Joshua 24:14, 15, "...choose for yourselves this day whom you will serve, whether the gods which your fathers served that were on the other side of the River, or the gods of the Amorites, in whose land you dwell. But as for me and my house, we will serve the Lord." We make many bad choices in our lifetimes, but Jesus through His blood can wipe the slate clean. You all also make many good choices, and our hope is that your number one choice is Jesus as Lord and Savior.

The good news of the Gospel of Jesus is that today you can start all over again. Luke 9:23 "Take up your cross daily."

Jesus made it all possible 2,000 years ago already.

It turns out that 'Ground Zero' is not the Garden of Eden, Pearl Harbor, New Mexico, New York City on 9/11, or any other place on Earth. It is Calvary. This is where our God sent His Only Son for your healing and forgiveness.

Romans 4:1 "So a person should think about us this way—as servants of Christ and managers of God's secrets."

Romans 16:25, 26 "May the glory be to God who can strengthen you with my good news and the message that I preach about Jesus Christ. He can strengthen you with the announcement of the secret that was kept quiet for a long time. Now that secret is revealed through what the prophets wrote. It is made known to the Gentiles in order to lead to their faithful obedience based on the command of the eternal God."

1 Corinthians 2:2, 6-10 "I had made up my mind not to think about anything while I was with you except Jesus Christ, and to preach him as crucified. We talk about God's wisdom, which has been hidden as a secret. God determined this wisdom in advance, before time began, for our glory. It is a wisdom that none of the present-day rulers have understood, because if they did understand it, they would never have crucified the Lord of glory!" But this is precisely what is written: "God has prepared things for those who love him that no eye has seen, or ear has heard, or that haven't crossed the heart/mind (καρδία) of any human

being. God has revealed these things to us through the Spirit. The Spirit searches everything, including the depths of God."

Romans 13:12 "Now we see a reflection in a mirror; then we will see face-to-face. Now I know partially, but then I will know completely in the same way that I have been completely known."

1 Corinthians 15:52 "Listen, I'm telling you a secret: All of us won't die, but we will all be changed."

Colossians 1:27 "God wanted to make the glorious riches of this secret plan known among the Gentiles, which is Christ living in you, the hope of glory."

E. G. White writes in *Education*, pages 169-172, *the Mysteries of the* Bible (Chapter 18) "No finite mind can fully comprehend the character or the works of the Infinite One. We cannot by searching find out God. To minds the strongest and most highly cultured, as well as to the weakest and most ignorant, that holy Being must remain clothed in mystery. But though "clouds and darkness are round about Him: righteousness and judgment are the foundation of His throne." Psalm 97:2, R.V. We can so far comprehend His dealing with us as to discern boundless mercy united to infinite power. We can understand as much of His purposes as we are capable of comprehending; beyond this we may still trust the hand that is omnipotent, the heart that is full of love."

Paul stressed the mysteries of God in his letters. It is almost as if Paul describes a secret, but that the answer is not hidden. However, it would never be known if God did not make it known. "In English a 'mystery' is something dark, obscure, secret, and puzzling. What is 'mysterious' is usually inexplicable or incomprehensible.

The Greek word *'mysterion'* is different, however. Although still a 'secret', it is no longer closely guarded but open. More simply, *mysterion* is a truth hitherto hidden from human knowledge or understanding but now disclosed by the revelation of God." (Stott)

"He made known to me the mystery." Paul did not hesitate to claim that the mystery he will reveal was given to him by revelation. But it was not given to only him by revelation. It was also given specifically to Peter by revelation (Acts 11:1-18), and it is consistent with prophecy in the Old Testament (such as Isaiah 49:6) and the specific words of Jesus (Acts 1:8).

In his letter to the Ephesians, Paul describes the Godhead's mysteries as the Creator's hidden design; as being planned from the beginning; God's secret plan about Jesus the Messiah and Savior; and this plan has two important elements:

† The Cross of Calvary - Colossians 1:27 "God wanted to make the glorious riches of this secret plan known among the Gentiles, which is Christ living in you, the hope of glory."

† The Gospel of Grace to all the world - Ephesians 3:6 "This plan is that the Gentiles would be coheirs and parts of the same body, and that they would share with the Jews in the promises of God in Christ Jesus through the gospel."

Ephesians 1:4-9 "God chose us in Christ to be holy and blameless in God's presence before the creation of the world. God destined us to be his adopted children through Jesus

Christ because of his love. This was according to his goodwill and plan and to honor his glorious grace that he has given to us freely through the Son whom he loves. We have been ransomed through his Son's blood, and we have forgiveness for our failures based on his overflowing grace, which he poured over us with wisdom and understanding. God revealed his hidden design to us, which is according to his goodwill and the plan that he intended to accomplish through his Son. This is what God planned for the climax of all times: to bring all things together in Christ, the things in heaven along with the things on earth."

Ephesians 3:2-12 "You've heard, of course, about the responsibility to distribute God's grace, which God gave to me for you, right? God showed me his secret plan in a revelation, as I mentioned briefly before (when you read this, you'll understand my insight into the secret plan about Christ). Earlier generations didn't know this hidden plan that God has now revealed to his holy apostles and prophets through the Spirit. This plan is that the Gentiles would be coheirs and parts of the same body, and that they would share with the Jews in the promises of God in Christ Jesus through the gospel. I became a servant of the gospel because of the grace that God showed me through the exercise of his power. God gave his grace to me, the least of all God's people, to preach the good news about the immeasurable riches of Christ to the Gentiles. God sent me to reveal the secret plan that had been hidden since the beginning of time by God, who created everything. God's purpose is now to show the rulers and powers in the heavens the many different varieties of his wisdom through the church. This was consistent (Jesus Christ the same yesterday, today and forever – Hebrews 13:8) with the plan he had from the beginning of time that he accomplished through Christ Jesus our Lord. In Christ we have bold and confident access to God through faith in him."

Ephesians 5:32 "This is a great mystery: but I speak concerning Christ and the church." (μέγας μυστήριον) Spanish: "*Grande es este misterio.*"

Ephesians 6:19 "As for me, pray that when I open my mouth, I'll get a message that confidently makes this secret plan of the gospel known."

Colossians 1:26, 27 "I'm completing it with a secret plan that has been hidden for ages and generations but which has now been revealed to his holy people. God wanted to make the glorious riches of this secret plan known among the Gentiles, which is Christ living in you, the hope of glory."

Colossians 2:2 "My goal is that their hearts would be encouraged and united together in love so that they might have all the riches of assurance that come with understanding, so that they might have the knowledge of the secret plan of God, namely Christ. All the treasures of wisdom and knowledge are hidden in him."

Colossians 2:6, 7 (The mystery of the Cross) "So live in Christ Jesus the Lord in the same way as you received him. Be rooted and built up in him, be established in faith, and overflow with thanksgiving just as you were taught. See to it that nobody enslaves you with philosophy and foolish deception, which conform to human traditions and the way the world thinks and acts rather than Christ. All the fullness of deity lives in Christ."

Colossians 4:3 "At the same time, pray for us also. Pray that God would open a door for the word so we can preach the secret (μυστήριον *mysterion*) plan of Christ, which is why I'm in chains."

"If those who today are teaching the word of God, would uplift the cross of Christ higher and still higher, their ministry would be far more successful. If sinners can be led to give one earnest look at the cross, if they can obtain a full view of the crucified Savior, they will realize the depth of God's compassion and the sinfulness of sin.

Christ's death proves God's great love for man. It is our pledge of salvation. To remove the cross from the Christian would be like blotting the sun from the sky. The cross brings us near to God, reconciling us to Him. With the relenting compassion of a father's love, Jehovah looks upon the suffering that His Son endured in order to save the race from eternal death, and accepts us in the Beloved.

Without the cross, man could have no union with the Father. On it depends our every hope. From it shines the light of the Savior's love, and when at the foot of the cross the sinner looks up to the One who died to save him, he may rejoice with fullness of joy, for his sins are pardoned. Kneeling in faith at the cross, he has reached the highest place to which man can attain." E. G. White, *The Acts of the Apostles*, pages 208, 209.

The following is a touching story. A grieving father's simple appeal to strangers resulted in a beautiful gift: portraits of his daughter, finally free of the machines that surrounded her during her brief life. The Ohio dad, whose baby died, posted a brief request on Reddit one weekend.

"My daughter recently passed away after a long battle in the children's hospital," he wrote. "Since she was in the hospital her whole life, we never were able to get a photo without all her tubes. Can someone remove the tubes from this photo?"

Nathen Steffel included a photo of his daughter Sophia and asked strangers for help in removing the tubes with photo editing software. The response was huge, with replies including beautifully retouched photos and even drawings for the grieving family.

Nathen Steffel, who posted the request, sent a brief statement on a website to tell other parents about the experience. "I didn't really want all the publicity, I just wanted a picture," Steffel wrote in an email. "What I received was a whole lot of love and support from complete strangers."

His daughter Sophia was born May 30 and lived just six weeks, he said. She died from complications from a liver tumor, he wrote. Steffel and his wife knew from the first ultrasound that something was wrong, but they did not realize how serious the situation was.

Their hearts were shattered when their baby died, but when they received the only picture of her with all the tubes and medical devices photo-shopped and removed, it was all that they had left and this gave them hope and healing.

Let us remember that the Bible is not only a story about someone else and it is not just about some other time. The Bible from Genesis to Revelation, is a book about God. It is also a book about the many men and women in the salvation history of God's people. It is the story told by forty Holy Spirit inspired authors during a period of nearly 1,700 years.

It is also a book about your life. Somewhere in these many pages you will find promises, healing, empowering, new life, redemption and the answers to many things in your life. It is a map of the landscape of your life now. It is a revelation, shining the light of awareness on all sides and facets of human experience and gives answers to what is happening to you now - the good and bad stories – and how these reveal our struggle, our identity and our moment. The message of the Cross and the soon Coming of the world's Redeemer brings hope and healing to each of our hearts and lives.

It is your choice to let the blood of Jesus wipe your life clean of all the sin and filth that does not belong.

The Cross of Jesus is the Key! Colossians 2:14 "By canceling the record of debt that stood against us with its legal demands. This he set aside, nailing it to the cross." ESV

1 Timothy 3:16 "Without question, the mystery of godliness is great: he was revealed as a human, declared righteous by the Spirit, seen by angels, preached throughout the nations, believed in around the world, and taken up in glory."

2 Thessalonians 2:7, 8 (*Prophecy of antichrist see 1 John 4:3*) "The hidden plan to live without any law is at work now, but it will be secret (μυστήριον ἀνομία *misteria anomia - mystery of lawlessness*) only until the one who is holding it back is out of the way. Then the person who is lawless will be revealed. The Lord Jesus will destroy him with the breath from his mouth. When the Lord comes, his appearance will put an end to him."

Yes, God loved the world, including you, so much, that he sent his only Son to die on the cruel Roman cross so that your live can be washed clean with the Blood of the Lamb.

You may have heard about Corrie ten Boom, read her books, or seen the movie *The Hiding Place* about her life in a Nazi concentration camp. Corrie and her family saved many hundreds of Jews during the Nazi occupation of Holland, hiding them in secret rooms in their house.

In 1944, Corrie was called before a Nazi judge.

"When I testified of my faith, the Lord touched the heart of that judge. And instead of an enemy, he became a friend. But he had to do his job. And so it happened that suddenly he showed me papers found in my house, and to my horror, I saw names, addresses, and particulars that could mean not only my death sentence, but the death sentence of my family and friends who were in prison."

"The judge said, "Can you explain these papers?" I said, "No I can't." And I felt terrible, terrible, unhappy."

"But he knew better than I how dangerous the papers were and he turned and opened the door of the stove and threw all the papers into the flames."

"My, how happy I was that moment. If you had told me that I could be 100 percent happy when I was in prison at the hands of an enemy, I should have never believed it. But when I saw the flames destroy these horrible papers it was as if for the first time I understood Colossians 2:13 and 14 where it is written that "God made you alive with Christ and forgave all your sins. He destroyed the record of the debt we owed, with its requirements that worked against us. He canceled it by nailing it to the cross."

10

Jesus: Creator, Lord and Savior

"Lift up Jesus, you that teach the people, lift Him up in sermon, in song, in prayer. Let all your powers be directed to pointing souls, confused, bewildered, lost to "the Lamb of God." Lift Him up, the risen Savior, and say to all who hear, Come to Him who "hath loved us, and hath given himself for us" (Ephesians 5:2). "Remove the cross from the Christian and it is like blotting out the sun which illumines the day, and dropping the moon and the stars out of the firmament of the heavens at night."
E.G. White, Our High Calling, p. 46

Surfing Facebook a while ago we found that someone sharing a verse from the book of Colossians, misspelt the name of the church as *Collisians*. Freudian slip?

The apostle Paul writes the letter to the Christians in Colossae, because there was already misinformation about what to believe and teach in the early Church. Paul clearly states the case that Jesus is our Creator, Lord and Savior. Unfortunately, many do not understand the central message of redemption that is outlined in this epistle. The words of Christ and the Cross as found in Colossians chapter 2 have resulted in many disputes, arguments, semantic juggling and lots of misunderstanding. Only prayer, the leading of the Holy Spirit, deep study, plus the ability to be able to give up enduring inaccuracies, can help us achieve consensus in the name of Jesus Christ.

The challenge for you is to be aware of old historic mistakes, wrong interpretations, and to grow in Christ, accepting newly revealed facts in more accurate translations. This is the work of the Holy Spirit, prayer, and faith. Old truths resurface because of the discovery of better Biblical manuscripts and more factual translations of Scriptural references.

Colossians 2:14 - KJV "Blotting out the handwriting of ordinances that was against us, which was contrary to us, and took it out of the way, nailing it to his cross." The traditional exposition of this verse is that the Ten Commandment law or the laws of ceremonies and sacrifices were nailed to the Cross, but this does not harmonize with the context, the central message of Colossians, or the major message of Paul in all his Epistles.

The 2011 Common English Bible reads: "He destroyed the record of the debt we owed, with its requirements that worked against us. He canceled it by nailing it to the cross."

Earlier in the chapter, in Colossians 2:2, Paul states his perception of God's secret plan: "My goal is that their hearts would be encouraged and united together in love so that they might have all the riches of assurance that come with understanding, so that they might have the knowledge of **the secret plan of God**, namely Christ." It is amazing that God through Paul can state the truth of salvation so clearly, and even though it is revealed as a secret plan, it is shared so endearingly that even a small child can grasp the meaning.

The Apostle Paul continues this passionate message in verse 17, where he confirms that Jesus' death on the Cross was the same moment that the curtains of the Temple Sanctuary were ripped open. This cancelled the Old Jewish Covenant of priests, rituals, sacrifices, festivals, and ceremonies. "Again Jesus cried out with a loud shout. Then he died. Look, the curtain of the sanctuary was torn in two from top to bottom. The earth shook, the rocks split." Mathew 27:50, 51

Paul reaches a conclusion to an argument that some of the early Christians had: "So don't let anyone judge you about eating or drinking or about a festival, a new moon observance, or sabbaths." Only Jesus is our Judge. This is confirmed in all the Word of God, in Psalm 22, the message of the Messianic Prophet Isaiah, in the Book of Daniel, and the letters of Paul.

E. G. White wrote "Let no one come to the conclusion that there is no more truth to be revealed. The diligent, prayerful seeker for truth will find precious rays of light yet to shine forth from the word of God." *Counsels on Sabbath School Work*, p. 34

"We have many lessons to learn, and many, many to unlearn. God and heaven alone are infallible. Those who think that they will never have to give up a cherished view, never have occasion to change an opinion, will be disappointed. In regard to infallibility, I never claimed it; God alone is infallible. His word is true, and in Him is no variableness, or shadow of turning." *Selected Messages, Book One*, pp. 416 and 37.

Most of us have been victimized, hurt and sinned against, and all of us have been either the perpetrator or persecutor of hurt to someone else. Our brokenness is from one or the other, from hurting other persons to being hurt yourself, from not being forgiven or not forgiving. This is the reason why God's one and only Son came as the Messiah Jesus to heal our brokenness and sin.

In God's words, Colossians 2:14 (Tyndale), "He cancelled the record that contained the charges against us. He took it and destroyed it by nailing it to Christ's cross." There is power in the Blood of the Lamb.

What, or who, was nailed to the cross? The answer is Jesus! Jesus was nailed to the cross and our sins with Him.

He paid for all our sins, He can forgive all the sins you have committed and heal the damage done by your sin and the sins of others. It is all summed up in that beautiful words Savior and Redeemer. Remember that Jesus is not your Savior until you ask Him, and by telling Him you are putting your total trust in Him.

Has there ever been a time when you have done that? That is the day the healing begins. It could be today for you. Tell the Lord you want Him to save you from sin and shame.

No one else has been able to put together all your broken pieces. That is why Jesus came to bind up the brokenhearted. He is your miracle. He is your hope of a new beginning. He is your wonderful hope of a happy ending. We sometimes need radical change, not just a quick fix. In this instant gratification, throwaway society, we do not enjoy having to fix things, but when we do try, we sometimes go to extremes, like the special prosecutor who spent twelve million dollars investigating a thirty-five-thousand-dollar crime!

This does not imply, suggest or teach a philosophy of imperfection. Nor is a gospel of unattainable legalistic faultlessness presented. We can all say, "I am an unfinished product. I am still under construction." Each new day there is a lot of room for grace and growth. Paul says in Romans 3:23, "For have all sinned and fall short of the glory of God." However, God declares us "Not Guilty" when we accept His Son Jesus Christ, the Messiah. The New Living Translation Isaiah 61:1 says "The Spirit of the Sovereign LORD is upon me, for the LORD has anointed me to bring good news to the poor. He has sent me to comfort the brokenhearted and to proclaim that captives will be released and prisoners will be freed."

The only perfect person who ever lived came from a bad neighborhood. Some of His ancestors were antisocial and criminal. He was born in a cow and sheep shed, and then His family fled and became refugees. He never owned much of his own, had to borrow a donkey, was tortured and murdered on the cross, and then buried in someone else's grave.

Through all of this, Jesus never blamed His background, His genetic inheritance, the poverty of His parents, or the occupation forces that ruled his country. He never complained that people were hurting His feelings, or that all His friends had left Him. Could anyone have had a deal rawer than that, and then come through it without deep depression, anxiety, substance addiction, homicidal tendencies, or a self-destructive psyche?

After forty days of fasting, Jesus was tempted with food from Satan, but he refused. How often have we all, when being well fed, after having regular meals, easily fall to the temptation of in-between chocolates and sugary drinks? The Lord lasted forty days, can we last forty minutes?

There is a challenge in Colossians 1:28, "Him we preach, warning every man and teaching every man in all wisdom, that we may present every man perfect in Christ Jesus." The experience of Christian perfection and maturity means daily growth and maturing in Jesus.

Jesus shares a spiritual secret in the parable of the two men praying when he says in Luke 18:9-14, "Two men went up to the temple to pray, one a Pharisee and the other a tax collector. The Pharisee stood and prayed thus with himself, 'God, I thank you that I am not like other men - extortionists, unjust, adulterers, or even as this tax collector. I fast twice a week; I give tithes of all that I possess.' And the tax collector, standing afar off, would not so much as raise his eyes to heaven, but beat his breast, saying, 'God, be merciful to me a sinner!' I tell you, this man went down to his house justified rather than the other; for everyone who exalts himself will be humbled, and he who humbles himself will be exalted."

The astonishing truth is that people that are really humble, do not even know it. Humility is to the possessor an imperceptible trait. Jesus is the King of Kings and Lord of Lords, yet He is the humblest person who ever lived. He really had something to be humble about, but never boasted about His riches, purity, power, or Divinity.

We all love mysteries and secrets. The New Testament contains a mystery, often wrongly interpreted, in 1 Corinthians 2:9. "However, as it is written: "No eye has seen, no ear has heard, no mind has conceived what God has prepared for those who love him" (NIV). Many different interpretations and opinions have been used to explain these words. The key is found when we understand that this is a passage taken out of the Old Testament from the book of the prophet Isaiah, known as the Messianic prophet.

Paul here refers to Isaiah 64:4: "Since ancient times no one has heard, no ear has perceived, no eye has seen any God besides you, who acts on behalf of those who wait for him." In the letter to the Corinthian church, Paul in chapter 2:2 gives the context of this statement "For I determined not to know anything among you except Jesus Christ and Him crucified." He repeats this in his salutation at the end of the letter to the church in Rome. Romans 16:25, 26 "Now to Him who is able to establish you according to my gospel and the preaching of Jesus Christ, according to the revelation of the mystery kept secret since the world began, but now made manifest, and by the prophetic Scriptures made known to all nations."

Paul sends the same message to the fledging church in Colossae. Colossians 1:25-27 "I became a servant of the church by God's commission, which was given to me for you, in order to complete God's word. I'm completing it with a secret plan that has been hidden for ages and generations but which has now been revealed to his holy people. God wanted to make the glorious riches of this secret plan[d] known among the Gentiles, which is Christ living in you, the hope of glory."

This secret or mystery that God prepared was His Only Son dying on the cruel Roman cross to set you free, and the opening of the way for both Jews and Gentiles to accept Jesus as Savior and Lord.

Acts 2:24 "But nothing, not even my life, is more important than my completing my mission. This is nothing other than the ministry I received from the Lord Jesus: to testify about the good news of God's grace."

There is a scarlet thread running through the Word of God. From Genesis through Revelation. The first two chapters of Genesis do not deal with sin and impending doom, and the final two chapters of Revelation do not deal with sin either. Everything in all the rest of the Christian Bible deals with the salvation history, prophecies of and promises to God's people.

It is also useful to see that the same crimson thread weaves through all of Paul's letters, as it does in the epistle to the Colossians. In the letter to the church at Colossae Paul writes in Colossians 2:2, 13 and 14:

† 2:2 "My goal is that their hearts (καρδία *kardia*) would be encouraged and united together in love so that they might have all the riches of assurance (πληροφορία *plērophoria*) that come with understanding (σύνεσις *synesis*) so that they might have the knowledge (ἐπίγνωσις *epignōsis*) of the secret plan (μυστήριον *mysterion*) of God, namely Christ.

† 2:13 "When you were dead in your sins and in the uncircumcision of your flesh, God made you alive with

Christ. He forgave us all our sins." **Sins** = (πᾶς παράπτωμα *pas paraptōma* - fault, offence, sin, trespass).

† 2:14 He destroyed (ἐξαλείφω *exaleiphō* obliterated, wiped out) the record (χειρόγραφον *cheirographon* handwritten note) of the debt (δόγμα *dogma* - doctrine, decree, ordinance) we owed, with its requirements (ὑπεναντίος *hypenantios*) that worked against (κατά *kata*) us. He canceled it (αἴρω αὐτός ἐκ μέσος *airō autos ek mesos* - He removed it out of the way) by nailing (προσηλόω *proseloō*) it to the cross (σταυρός *stauros*)."

Sometimes the Shakespearian language of the King James Version of 1611 tends to be ponderous and difficult. This leads to interpretations that do not always harmonize with the rest of Scripture. No belief or interpretation can be validated by using only one Bible version or translation. We need to read different Bibles, and maybe get someone to explain the original languages, especially to understand different words.

What all these hopeful, heartfelt and inspiring words in Colossians 2:14 really say is that **Jesus was nailed to the cross and took our sins there, wiping out the records of our sins from the book of death.** The plain and simple message that Paul writes in Colossians is that our Savior Lord Jesus gave up his life to free us from sin. Jesus, through the Grace of his Father, cancels the IOU or record of our sins. This is not a reference to any law or Biblical teaching nailed to the Cross. God's moral law is everlasting.

When Jesus, the Lamb of God, the sacrifice for our sins, died on that bad Friday, a strange event took place in the Temple. The curtain dividing the Most Holy Place from the Holy Place was ripped from top to bottom, opening the way to the mysterious emblems of that signified salvation to the Jewish people.

This ushered in a new age of God's grace and mercy.

No more Passover was needed.

No more Passover Lamb.

No more priestly or high priestly service.

No more feast days of the Old Testament that looked forward to the Coming of the Messiah.

Jesus is the Lamb, the Life, the Light, the Bread, and he became our High Priest.

The Common English Bible (CEB) is one of the most recent Bible translations (2011), which uses the same manuscripts as the original KJV. Even though the CEB has a few of its own slants, we found that when using it for the version to read for daily devotions and time with God, reading it gave faith and strength for the day ahead, as well as deepening the Grace of God in our hearts and minds. The English flows well, is beautiful and inspiring. We do not agree with all the renderings, but the same goes for any translation of the Scriptures.

The introduction to this Bible reads: "The Common English Bible (CEB) is not simply a revision or update of an existing translation. It is a bold new translation designed to meet the needs of Christians as they work to build a strong and meaningful relationship with God through Jesus Christ. A key goal of the translation team was to make the Bible accessible to a broad range of people; it's written at a comfortable level for over half of all English readers. As the translators did their work, reading specialists working with seventy-seven reading groups from more than a dozen denominations (including SDA's) review the texts to ensure a smooth and natural reading experience. Easy readability can enhance church worship and participation, and personal Bible study. It also encourages children and youth to discover the Bible for themselves, perhaps for the very first time." (From the Preface, CEB)

Colossians 2:14 Reveals that the Key that Unlocks Mysteries and Secrets is the Cross:

"He destroyed the record of the debt we owed, with its requirements that worked against us. He cancelled it by nailing it to the Cross." This translation makes the veracity, reality and power of the cross so much easier to grasp and understand.

Fundamentalist Christian churches have long used a superficial argument against God's seventh day Sabbath. They insist that Colossians 2:14 proclaims that the law was nailed to the Cross – and Adventists answer yes, but it was the Ceremonial Law of sacrifices and feast days - but we are all wrong. **The truth is that Jesus was nailed to the cross, and there he cleansed and wiped out the record of our repented and confessed sins with his precious blood.**

Ask yourself who or what was nailed to the Cross?

The answer is JESUS!

Jesus the Son of God and Son of Man was nailed to the Cross to wipe our sins out of the books of death (Daniel 7:10; Revelation 22:12).

The Old Testament laws and festivals that applied to Israel of old, became redundant and canceled when the

Temple curtain was torn in two from top to bottom, the same Friday afternoon that Jesus died – revealing the priesthood of Jesus Christ and all believers (1 Peter 2:5; Hebrews 2:17; 4:14, 15; 7:27; Revelation 1:6). Now we do not need priests or sacrifices or pilgrimages to Jerusalem any more. Our Lord Jesus is our Priest and High Priest, and also our sacrifice. You can give your heart, mind and behavior anytime and anywhere. Jesus is our Passover Lamb and the Bread of life.

Instead of shaking us – these revised and corrected interpretations should lead us to a closer and more meaningful walk with Jesus.

One of the greatest lessons that we can learn in our lives, is that we do not know everything. Therefore, determine to read your Bible immersed in the grace and love of God. Do not be a stranger to new light and deeper perceptions, especially as we study the Word of God. There are many so-called truths that we have inherited from our predecessors, but remember that they grew in Christ and passed on the torch and new light that they had.

Colossians 2:16 is correct when it says "Let no one judge you." This is because Jesus is my only Judge, and the seventh day Sabbath is the only Bible Sabbath, day of rest and worship mentioned in the Bible.

These verses in Colossians do not do away with God's weekly day of rest, the Sabbath. It has always been there.

Before any Jews. Before Sinai. It was the day that Jesus kept, that all the apostles kept, and the early Christian church worshipped on. Towards the end of time, more Bible secrets and truths will be revealed to us.

In Colossians 3 Paul shares his passionate life-changing experience, which dramatically led to his spiritual journey with the Lord Jesus Christ. He says in verse 4: "When Christ, who is your life, is revealed, then you also will be revealed with him in glory."

Then in verses 5-9 he describes the lifestyle of ignorance and sinfulness that sounds very much like a confession of his early life: "So put to death the parts of your life that belong to the earth, such as sexual immorality, moral corruption, lust, evil desire, and greed (*which is idolatry*). You used to live this way, when you were alive to these things. But now set aside these things, such as anger, rage, malice, slander, and obscene language. Don't lie to each other."

In the following verses 10-17 Paul describes the miracle of complete personality and temperament change. This sounds like turning into a new life direction, and enjoying a new life in Jesus Christ: "Take off the old human nature with its practices and put on the new nature, which is renewed in knowledge by conforming to the image of the one who created it. In this image, there is neither Greek nor Jew, circumcised nor uncircumcised, barbarian, Scythian, slave nor free, but Christ is all things and in all people. But now set aside these things, such as anger, rage, malice, slander, and obscene language. Don't lie to each other."

I have an earnest belief that as we open the secrets and mysteries of the Scriptures we will find, for example, that if Augustine was alive today he would not be Catholic, Luther would not be a Lutheran, the Wesley's would not be Wesleyan, and so we also need to be developing and growing in the light of 1844, 1884, and contemporary Christian growth. Which or whose church would Jesus be coming to on Sabbath?

The Bible Timeline of Redemption

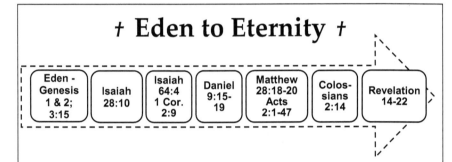

✝ Eden to Eternity ✝

| Eden - Genesis 1 & 2; 3:15 | Isaiah 28:10 | Isaiah 64:4 1 Cor. 2:9 | Daniel 9:15-19 | Matthew 28:18-20 Acts 2:1-47 | Colos-sians 2:14 | Revelation 14-22 |

Jesus' sacrifice on the Cross of Calvary is the central message and focus of the Bible. The Blood of our Messiah the Lord Jesus flows through all the Word of God like a scarlet thread from Genesis to Revelation.
The Cross is God's Key of Grace That unlocks many secrets and mysteries.

11

Serendipity

Revelation 14

"The cross of Calvary challenges, and will finally vanquish every earthly and hellish power. In the cross all influence centers, and from it all influence goes forth. It is the great center of attraction; for on it Christ gave up His life for the human race." E.G. White

September 11, 2001… as the buildings of the World Trade Center burst in anger and hate, firefighters, police and office workers who were still alive found the world collapsing around them. Dust, debris, and darkness surrounded them. Many thought this was the end, but some miraculously made it out alive. Dirty, disheveled, disbelieving and disheartened they struggled through the apocalyptic gloom, confusion and chaos. When the last few managed to get out alive, they were asked, "How did you get out?" Often the answer was, "I walked towards the light."

This was a day when ordinary people did extraordinary things. Heroism, bravery, courage, valor, fearlessness – these are some of the many words that describe the actions of countless people that day. Candles were lit at the terror sites, at the World Trade Center, the Pentagon and the Pennsylvania field. All over the world, people wept for and honored the nearly 3,000 persons who died. The lives of more than 30,000 persons saved, many of them injured, were also remembered. These were the workers, employees, bosses, visitors and rescue personnel who got out in time or were carried out in time. It was a remarkable miracle that so many were saved and were given the opportunity to see the sunshine again.

The last book in the Christian Bible, the Revelation of Jesus, is a light at the end of the tunnel of this present life on Earth. John wrote this final message from God, inspired by the Holy Spirit, as a Revelation of Jesus, not just a Revelation of history and prophecy.

What gives us strength, is the knowledge that we have a light available to us at all times and all places. The light of the Apocalypse is Jesus Christ, our Creator, Redeemer, and Messiah. John 8:12: Then Jesus spoke to them again, saying, "I am the light of the world. He who follows Me shall not walk in darkness, but have the light of life."

To get a good grasp and understanding of the Apocalypse, we need to utilize the same key that we used to decode all of the Scriptures. This is the Cross of Jesus. The key is the Gospel message of the Cross, of Jesus as Lord, Creator, Savior and Redeemer.

The book of Revelation also contains secrets and mysteries. Apart from being a right brained book of events, prophecies, symbols and history, the Apocalypse is basically another Gospel of Jesus. In the words of this Revelation we find comfort for our hearts and lives.

There are many times in our lives that we come across something that we have never seen, heard, smelled or touched before. Or make a discovery of a something that we did not even know existed. Even when we read our Bible we often find a precious nugget that we had not noticed before. This includes reading through the Bible, or a more goal directed study of a verse, chapter or book.

The reason why diamonds are mounted in gold or silver settings, is to enhance the security, context and splendor of the exquisite jewel. Move it around or turn it, and you will see new facets of color and beauty.

There are even 'aha' or 'wow' moments when something we have read in the Scriptures many times, takes on a whole new meaning, especially when you read a different version or translation.

This is what serendipity means. The unexpected discovery of something new and unexpected.

This same expectation is present when the spiritually hungry seeker looks at the Word of God with a prayerful open heart and mind, hoping for growing faith, joy and light around every corner. Even born-again Christians will always have something new to learn, old faults to delete, and deeper spirituality to enjoy. We never stop growing in Jesus Christ. The prophet Malachi promises that God will "open all the windows of the heavens for you and empty out a blessing until there is enough." Malachi 3:10.

In human thought, we need to establish priorities, meanings, and methods. Many good words and meanings have been hijacked by popular songs, greedy politicians and superficial opinions. We all need to set our world views to establish common ground for deliberating the Scriptures. For example, how do we see the Word of God? Is it completely verbally inspired? Is it just a compilation of books that contain the history of God's people and salvation? Or did God inspire the prophets, writers, disciples, apostles with His truthful messages, but they used their own verbal and writing skills? Even Bible translations and versions in different languages have misprints, mistakes or mistranslations.

There is a very important reason why King James of England had the Scriptures translated into English in 1611. In the introduction to older editions, the following words are penned *in order to warn off the interpretations of other men that dismay us*: "So that if on the one side, we shall be traduced by Popish Persons at home or abroad who therefore will malign us, because we are poor instruments to make God's Holy Truth to be yet more and more know..."

History tells us about the friction between Protestant England and Catholic Rome. Just six years before the 2011 release of the KJV, in 1605, a Papal terror plot was foiled when a plan to bomb the house of parliament with the King and all in it was discovered, and the perpetrators rounded up and hanged. Somehow God had his hand in safeguarding this great KJV translation and the Protestant King that eventually brought the Gospel to the whole world.

Following are some suggested ways for sorting out our dilemmas and questions in Bible study and research:
- Pray before you open God's Word
- Ask for the Leading of the Holy Spirit
- Radical Thought: the original meaning of the word 'radical' is the **root meaning** or going back to the roots. Many generations have abused, misused, misaligned and misapplied intended meanings.
- Develop honest hearts
- Have open and willing minds
- Check on the context and syntax
- Read the Bible in different translations and languages where possible.
- Remember that the Truths found in the Word of God are ageless, not open to personal bias, or used as snake oil to enrich oneself. The Bible is really a Book of Worship. Worship of God the Father, the Son of God and the Holy Spirit.
- The Bible Only: *Where do out beliefs come from?* Leroy Edwin Froom – Review and Herald Publishing Ass., Washington, D.C. 20012, 1971 p 107 - "No MAJOR doctrinal truth or prophetic interpretation of the Advent Faith was initially introduced among us through the agency of the Spirit of Prophecy - that is, through the instrumentality of Ellen White. That was never the design, or purpose, or sphere, of the operation of the Spirit of Prophecy. That was not God's method for the introduction of basic doctrinal truth into the Church of the Remnant."
- Be prepared and delight in serendipitous discovery

"Let no one come to the conclusion that there is no more truth to be revealed. The diligent, prayerful seeker for truth will find precious rays of light yet to shine forth from the word of God." E.G. White, *Counsels on Sabbath School Work,* p. 34

Remember that valuable Bible Study for a seeker includes: being prayer driven; Spirit led; open minded; and an honest heart.

Beliefs about the Second Coming of Jesus Christ are often centered on believers expecting the Lord in their time. The Bible says no person knows the hour, always have a fervent hope of it being soon. Even Paul writes in the well-known Hebrews 11:39, 40, after his long list of persons who have died in faith and rested in their graves, that "All these people did not receive what was promised, though they were given approval for their faith. God provided something better for us so they would not be made perfect without us." Paul tells us that all the righteous will be resurrected at the same time, hopefully during his life.

The Baptist preacher William Miller, proclaimed that Jesus would come in 1844, but those who followed him were deeply disappointed. After this terrible disappointment of 1844, several Bible study groups were organized. During this time of revival, fervent prayer, intense study of God's Word, and the leading of the Holy Spirit, these Bible study groups decided to go back to God's original Gospel as taught in the Bible, to find out what God wanted them to do next. The first three angels' messages of Revelation 14 had a significant effect on these early Adventist believers.

Revelation 14 – The Message of the Cross: The Angels of Revelation 14 have key messages for the serious times we are living in today. Angels are messengers from God. The messages of the angels of Revelation 14 were prayerfully studied by Christians in the early Advent movement during the middle of the nineteenth century. The powerful gospel messages of the first three angels made a big impact on many Christians who had been misled by the Baptist preacher that proclaimed that Jesus Advent would be in 1844. They continued in study groups that focused on end time prophecies and the meaning of the Gospel message.

"We have many lessons to learn, and many, many to unlearn. God and heaven alone are infallible. Those who think that they will never have to give up a cherished view, never have occasion to change an opinion, will be disappointed. In regard to infallibility, I never claimed it; God alone is infallible. His word is true, and in Him is no variableness, or shadow of turning." E.G. White, *Selected Messages*, Book One, p. 416.

The Angels' Messages of Revelation 14:6-20 were made with powerful loud voices (μέγας φωνή *megas phōnē*), and included proclamations that the time has come for the Everlasting Gospel to be preached (14:6, 7); for God's people to come out of Babylon (14:8); and for the Commandments of God and the faith of Jesus (14:9-13) to be proclaimed.

The first step in decoding the messages of Revelation is to read the context prayerfully. The following uses the 2011 translation of the Common English Bible.

Global Gospel Messages of
The First Three Angels

1. Revelation 14:6, 7 "Then I saw **another angel** flying high overhead with eternal good news to proclaim to those who live on earth, and to every nation, tribe, language, and people. He said in a loud voice, "Fear God and give him glory, for the hour of his judgment has come. Worship the one who made heaven and earth, the sea and springs of water."

2. Revelation 14:8 "**Another angel**, a second one, followed and said, "Fallen, fallen is Babylon the great! She made all the nations drink the wine of her lustful passion."

3. Revelation 14:9-11 "Then **another angel**, a third one, followed them and said in a loud voice, "If any worship the beast and its image, and receive a mark on their foreheads or their hands, they themselves will also drink the wine of God's passionate anger and wrath."

Revelation 14:12 then identifies God's Christians at the end of time as those who proclaim these messages *"This calls for the endurance of the saints, who keep God's commandments and keep the faith Jesus."*

The Second Advent of Jesus:
Three More Angels' Messages

Revelation 14:14 "Then I looked, and there was a white cloud. On the cloud was seated someone who looked like the Son of Man. He had a gold crown on his head and a sharp sickle in his hand."

4. Revelation 14:15, 16 "**Another angel** came out of the temple, calling in a loud voice to the one seated on the cloud: "Use your sickle to reap the harvest, for the time to

harvest has come, and the harvest of the earth is ripe." So the one seated on the cloud swung his sickle over the earth, and the earth was harvested."

5.   Revelation 14:17 "Then **another angel** came out of the temple in heaven, and he also had a sharp sickle."

6.   Revelation 14:18, 19 "Still **another angel**, who has power over fire, came out from the altar. He said in a loud voice to the one who had the sharp sickle, "Use your sharp sickle to cut the clusters in the vineyard of the earth, because its grapes are ripe." So the angel swung his sickle into the earth, and cut the vineyard of the earth, and he put what he reaped into the great winepress of God's passionate anger."

There is a common denominator in each of these six messages, and that is that each is identified as **another angel**. Angels are messengers of God. The early Adventists took it to heart that God had given these Gospel messages of the Apocalypse especially for the time that they lived in. This was the time of great preachers, the Industrial Revolution, the time of extreme Bible critics in Europe, and the time of the academic rise of the theories of Evolution that countered God's Word in Genesis.

Was it coincidence that at the same time, during the middle of the nineteenth century, Charles Darwin was researching his concepts of evolution? Some decades later Marx and Engels based their economic and political philosophies on the theory of evolution, and on the survival of the fittest. The Industrial Revolution was gaining impetus, and the world was standing at the threshold of the modern age.

The nineteenth century became the time that the world was turning its back on the Creator God, and on Jesus as our only Mediator. The world needed The Gospel message to remind people of Jesus as Lord and Savior. During the second half of the 1800's there was intense study on the unveiling, unsealing, opening, and proclaiming of the apocalyptic gospel messages of Revelation 14. At the General Conference of Adventists in 1888, there was some confusion as to what the emphasis of Bible study, preaching, teaching and evangelism should be. This was a great time to get out of the straight jacket of legalism and for this young Protestant church to establish the centrality of Jesus as Lord and Savior, and His Cross that opened the Gospel of grace to all humans.

"Many had lost sight of Jesus. They needed to have their eyes directed to His divine person, His merits, and His changeless love for the human family. All power is given into His hands, that He may dispense rich gifts unto men, imparting the priceless gift of His own righteousness to the helpless human agent.

The uplifted Saviour is to appear in His efficacious work as the Lamb slain, sitting upon the throne, to dispense the priceless covenant blessings, the benefits He died to purchase for every soul who should believe on Him. John could not express that love in words; it was too deep, too broad; he calls upon the human family to behold it. The uplifted Saviour is to appear in His efficacious work as the Lamb slain, sitting upon the throne, to dispense the priceless covenant blessings, the benefits He died to purchase for every soul who should believe on Him. John could not express that love in words; it was too deep, too broad; he calls upon the human family to behold it. say that Seventh-day Adventists talk the law, the law, but do not teach or believe Christ." recorded in *Testimonies to Ministers*, p 92.

For the Christian Church the cry went out to come out of Babylon, out of confusion and heresy, into the wonderful salvation, freedom and grace of Jesus our Savior; accepting the Bible as our only source of doctrine; the true church as Jesus' community; God's people are a people of love, patience, obedience and faith in Jesus; there is a final Judgment at the end of time; and Jesus is coming soon to set up His Kingdom of Glory.

Some Bible versions seem a little vague about the number of angels in this chapter, but a careful analysis of the original words and language used, we find that there are in fact six angels who *speak with a loud voice*.

Why is there no seventh Angel? All other prophetic lists in the Apocalypse have seven Angels, trumpets and other lists. Maybe we can add a seventh message (but not from an Angel) as a homiletic endeavor with a final challenge to all hearers. There are more than 50 other lists of 7 in the book of Revelation. Why not chapter in 14?

Revelation 12:14 has a clear message that the Second Advent or Coming of Jesus takes place after the messages of the first three Angels have been proclaimed in all the world. "Then I looked, and there was a white cloud. On the cloud was seated someone who looked like the Son of Man. He had a gold crown on his head and a sharp sickle in his hand."

The messages of the final 3 Angels take place in quick succession, but there is no 7th Angel.

At the time when the seventh angel should be giving a message, chapter 14 instead ends abruptly. At the end of this prophecy, to fit in with the other six progressive sections in this chapter, it is not the loud voice of an angel messenger, but we find that prophetically and chronologically the voice of the Creator Himself, our Savior, the Lord Jesus Christ, saying "IT IS FINISHED!"

The final Divine proclamation 'IT IS FINISHED' (*completed*) is proclaimed at least 3 times in prophetic and salvation history of the Scriptures:

1. At the end of Creation, Genesis 2:1, 'It is Finished!'

2. At Redemption on the Cross of Calvary, John 19:30 'It is Finished!'

3. At the end of time (Revelation 16:17) the seventh angel proclaims 'It is Finished!'

Revelation 14 takes us to the end of time, the final message of God for this Earth's present history. Later Revelation 21 and 22, it takes us all the way to Heaven, the New Earth and the New Jerusalem.

The Second Coming of Jesus and preparing the Christian church for this ultimate event became the focal message of early Advent believers, but we need to be aware that there are more than just three angel messengers in Revelation 14:6-20. These messages are also important and are proclaimed as part of the Gospel of Jesus before the end of time.

One problem for past commentators, was that they mostly used the King James Version with its often laborious word choice and sentence construction in the book of Revelation.

With all the many signs at the end of time, there is one important and substantial sign that identifies the end of time. In Matthew 24:14 Jesus says in His own words "And this gospel of the kingdom will be preached in all the world as a witness to all the nations, and then the end will come." It is important that we know the signs of Jesus Coming. The Bible does not tell us the day or date, but it is vital to be prepared and have a personal relationship with Jesus as your Lord, Creator and Savior.

Revelation 14 is a summary of the Gospel truths that are proclaimed at the end of time. In this chapter, we find the Christian Gospel includes worship of the Creator God, coming out of the Babylon of sin and confusion, proclaiming the Gospel of Grace, the importance of the Commandments of God, the Final Prophetic events, and the Second Advent.

The crucial dynamic is that these core messages still need to be shouted from the rooftops today! This includes corporate worship, radio, TV, social media, cyber space, and any other way that the Love of God can be shared. They constitute the Gospel message that the Christian church needs to be proclaiming today. Acts 4:12 "Salvation is found in no one else, for there is no other name under heaven given to men by which we must be saved."

Revelation 14 uses amazing didactic methods, and is a summary of the whole Apocalypse, especially the chapters 15-22 that ensue. The central teachings of the Christian church are worship, redemption, promises, warnings and prophecies. It tells all who choose to get out of Babylon and its teachings, including Babylonian sun worship or Sunday worship, and preparing for the second Coming of the Messiah.

The Protestant Reformation of the 16th century was revived and gained impetus in the 19th century. This was a time of great preachers such as the Wesleys, Spurgeon and

Murray. At the same time that Darwin published the Origin of the Species, diamonds and gold were discovered in America and South Africa, the Industrial Revolution started, transport was moving at faster speeds, and God had a message. Missionaries trekked to Africa and the Far East. Revival and reformation was experienced by thousands of persons.

The twentieth century was one of the greatest times for the Christian Church in general. New denominations were organized, missions, hospitals and schools grew like mushrooms on all the continents and islands. Christianity became the largest religion in the world. The two World Wars that raged led many back to church revivals and a renewal of faith and worship.

Following is a summary of the final warning messages to this dying world: the preaching of the Everlasting Gospel in the last days explicitly includes: worship God as Creator; come out of Babylon; enjoy a lifestyle of Freedom and Grace; be faithful and obedient to God and keep the Faith of Jesus; proclaim the soon Coming of Jesus; and get ready for the Kingdom of God, and then the final judgement. These are the imperatives of the Gospel of Jesus for the last days.

Even though these vital messages of the first three Angels are proclaimed globally, worldwide more people than ever are leaving God out of their lives, out of their homes, out of their sciences, and out of their politics. Secular humanism, materialism, liberalism and an easy Gospel are taking over. It seems that the center of the earlier and post millennial generations Y and Z is 'I' – back to the selfish, egoistic lifestyles of the 1920's, 1960's and 2,000's.

The Messages of Revelation 14 Include:

➤ **3 Angels' Messages – 6-13**
~ *God's Final Gospel Message – Worship God*
1. The Everlasting Gospel - verses 6, 7
2. Babylon is Fallen – God's Grace – 8
3. The Word of God and Faith of Jesus - 9-12

➤ **Advent of Jesus Christ – 14:14**

➤ **Next 3 Angels' Messages – 15-19**
~ *God's Final Harvest – New Jerusalem*
4. The Final Harvest - 15, 16
5. God's People Saved - 17
6. Judgment of the Wicked - 18, 19

7. **"IT IS FINISHED!"** – 16:17; 22:16, 17

The Three Angels' messages of Revelation 14:6-12, and the final three angels in verses 13 to 20 constitute God's final appeal to the world just before Christ's Second Advent. Here is a call to worship the true God. The completion of the great commission to preach the gospel to all nations preceding the Savior's return is also significant for this time, as well as the reward for the righteous, and the punishment for the wicked. This chapter still contains a challenge, hope and prophetic victory in Jesus. Revelation 14:12 "Here is the patience of the saints; here are those who keep the commandments of God and the faith of Jesus."

Only when the great charge and Christian urgency to preach this Gospel to all the world has been carried out, Christ will return. Complete Bible truth is to be preached, but God has a special warning and appeal in the final messages of these angels. The angels' messages bring into focus the great issues of the last days, the gospel, the Sabbath, the judgment, and the true worship of the Creator God. Our churches should be the place where folks come to worship, praise and celebrate, not by copying the latest fads, popular music of social gospel, but to share our Father in Heaven, Jesus the Messiah, and the power of the Holy Spirit. This threefold message of Revelation 14 is the unifying factor that lends special present day significance proclaiming the hope, grace, care and love God to a World's needy, starved and thirsty population.

One of the greatest problems today is that the protest has left Protestants! The Christian church has become the tail-light instead of the head-light of the world. One pastor said that wherever Paul went there was revival, but wherever he goes, he drinks tea!

The time is here! The time for revival and reformation! Remember that Christian revival is always Christ centered and Bible based. This is the challenge of the Apocalypse.

Finally: We would love to see our Churches holding on to their spirituality, worship and prophetic heritage, and empowering members and leaders to carry on with the Gospel message in the Adventist Protestant Context.

One thing more – our church is a Church of Worship. At the end of Creation, the last day, the seventh day, God created a day of rest and worship. After the flood, Noah and his family worshiped the Creator God. The first of the Ten Commandments is a commandment of Worship. The first of the Three Angel's Messages in Revelation 14, is a message of coming back to the Worship of the true God. Our faith in God the Father, God the Son, and God the Holy Spirit needs to be paramount. Many Christian churches have changed from the centrality of the pulpit and Bible in preaching, to a stage for entertainment and motivational preaching. Or the altar and Eucharist where Christ is sacrificed thousands of times each day in legalistic liturgical litanies.

An Urgent Appeal: The significant Bible verses discussed in these pages should not let us lose faith in Christianity or the Advent Movement. Any truthful and fresh reading of the Word of God should strengthen our belief and faith, and lead to a deeper and more meaningful walk with God. It should give deeper meaning and provide a firm footing for our fundamental beliefs. In fact, I believe that the explanations shared in this paper should remove a lot of prejudice and wrong opinions, and enable a deeper, uncomplicated, and well-defined communication of our heartfelt Christian beliefs.

The main Bible sections discussed, Isaiah 28:10, 64:4, 1 Corinthians 2:9, Colossians 2:14, and Revelation 14, are significant components of the scarlet thread of Jesus' Blood that flows through the Word of God from Genesis to Revelation, and then into our lives, hearts and minds. We are not changing any teachings or beliefs. Our greatest reply to doubters should be *Jesus and Him Crucified*.

After Colossians 2:14 God says *"let no person judge you."* Yes, Jesus is our only Judge and not any human. Colossians 3:17 "Whatever you do, whether in speech or action, do it all in the name of the Lord Jesus and give thanks to God the Father through him." This has always been the message of the Seventh-day Adventist Church, in the 1,800s, and in the twentieth, and twenty first century.

Some years ago, I baptized the Pastor (*Captain*) of a Salvation Army Church in a large city. Her testimony that she shared with us was "Now I know Jesus better than I have ever known Him before." This is what we should be doing – leading folks to delight in the grace and mercy of a loving God.

This book, all the chapters, all the questions and all the answers will never be complete until Jesus comes again. There will be born-again and passionate speakers, writers, authors and lecturers plus other people, who will share what God gives to them. So get on your knees. Open your heart and mind. Let God's Spirit speak through you.

We live in a world and time where people still want truth, honesty and openness. This must be an important part of any church, worship, evangelistic, healing and teaching ministry. To tell the truth about Jesus. To share the Gospel of the Cross and Jesus coming again. To proclaim the message of Revelation 3:20.

The Mysteries of God: It is amazing that the Bible book that frequently speaks about secrets and mysteries of God, is called the Unveiling, Opening, Revealing or Revelation. The final Gospel invitation is given to individuals and churches at the end of time (the Laodiceans). In Revelation 3:19 and 20 we read: "I correct and discipline those whom I love. So be earnest and change your hearts and lives. Look! I AM standing at the door and knocking. If any hear my voice and open the door, I will come in to be with them, and will have dinner with them, and they will have dinner with me."

We are told that the fastest way to spread a secret is to whisper it in someone's ear. It will then spread like wild fire. These days all you need to is to Tweet or Facebook and within a day or two it could reach millions, especially if you say it is a secret.

In Revelation 10:7 we read "In the days when the seventh angel blows his trumpet, God's mysterious (Greek *mysterion*) purpose will be accomplished, fulfilling the good news he gave to his servants the prophets." What is significant, is that the Apocalypse or Revelation (*Revealing*) references many secrets and mysteries, but much of this has not reached the lives, hearts and minds of billions of people on this planet. In fact, in Matthew 24:14 we read "This gospel of the kingdom will be proclaimed throughout the world as a testimony to all the nations. Then the end will come." Matthew 28:19 invites greater involvement of Christians as the final sign of the end of time as we know it "Therefore, go and make disciples of all nations, baptizing them in the name of the Father and of the Son and of the Holy Spirit, teaching them to obey everything that I've commanded you. Look, I myself will be with you every day until the end of this present age."

John, inspired by the Deity, authored the book of Revelation while a prisoner on the Island of Patmos, approximately 85-95 A.D. He mostly reveals prophetic events, the majority (six out of seven?) of which have already and historically been fulfilled. He writes messages of encouragement and hope for all Christians looking forward to end-time events, and warns about the Final Judgment of those persons who do not have the faith to accept Jesus as their personal Savior.

In Revelation 1:3 John writes about blessings for those who accept the Word of God: "Blessed is he who reads and those who hear the words of the prophecy, and heed the things which are written in it; for the time is near."

In Revelation chapters 1-3 John describes how and why he received these Apocalyptic messages, or the unveiling from God. Then in chapters 4 to 20 he describes the how and when of visions, which he received describing historical and prophetic outcomes. He describes Jesus as the Slain Lamb. Then in the final chapters of Revelation 21 and 22, we see scenes at the end of time on this Earth, of where God's saints will be. The Revelation finally ends with an invitation for the Messiah Jesus to come ASAP.

In Revelation chapter 10, the seventh Angel messenger announces that there will no longer be a delay, as with the sounding of the final and seventh trumpet the mysteries of God shall have been completed. Many commentaries say that this final Angel is Jesus Christ personally.

Whereas the last book of the Bible, the Revelation of Jesus, refers to many mysteries and secrets of God, this is in fact a continuation of the major messages of the Old Testament prophets. The prophet Isaiah in chapter 55:8 and 9, proclaims what God's message is for us during these final days on Earth, "For my thoughts are not your thoughts, neither are your ways my ways, saith the LORD. For as the heavens are higher than the earth, so are my ways higher than your ways, and my thoughts than your thoughts."

The Revelation unveils these final messages to a dying world, loudly proclaiming the finality of the Gospel Message, with trumpet sound. Revelation 11:15 "Then the seventh angel blew his trumpet (salpizo – the King James version says sounded), and there were loud voices in heaven saying, "The kingdom of the world has become the kingdom of our Lord and his Christ, and he will rule forever and ever."

If you want to unlock the *mysterions* of the Lord's messages for you, open the door of your heart.

The majestic sound and fanfare of trumpets celebrates, announces and broadcasts the momentous unveiling of Bible mysteries, in the hearts and minds of God's saved persons. This is the final grand celebration of those persons ready for stepping into the Everlasting Covenant with Jesus.

Revelation 10:5-7 "Then the angel I saw standing on the sea and on the land raised his right hand to heaven. He swore by the one who lives forever and always, who created heaven and what is in it, the earth and what is in it, and the sea and what is in it, and said, "The time is up. In the days when the seventh angel blows his trumpet, God's mysterious purpose will be accomplished, fulfilling the good news he gave to his servants the prophets."

The ABC's of the Gospel of Jesus:

All have sinned and come short of the Glory of God. Romans 3:23

Behold the Lamb of God, who takes away the sin of the world. John 1:29

Come to me, all of you who are weary and carry heavy burdens, and I will give you rest. Matthew 11:28

John 3:16, 17

"God so loved the world that he gave his only Son, so that everyone who believes in him won't perish but will have eternal life. God didn't send his Son into the world to judge the world, but that the world might be saved through him."

Ephesians 2:8

"For by grace you have been saved through faith, and that not of yourselves; it is the gift of God, not of works, lest anyone should boast."

Andrew Murray - Jesus' Blood

"The blood of Jesus is the greatest mystery of eternity, the deepest mystery of divine wisdom. Let us not imagine that we can easily grasp its meaning. God thought 4,000 years necessary to prepare men for it, and we also must take time, if we are to gain a knowledge of the power of the blood."

E. G. White – The Cross

"The sacrifice of Christ, as the atonement for sin is the great truth around which every other truth clusters. Every truth in the word of God, from Genesis to Revelation, in order to be rightly understood and appreciated, must be studied from the light that streams from the Cross of Calvary."

Free Book
"Steps to Christ"

Do you know Jesus, or do you only know about Him? This popular little book was written by Ellen White who knew Jesus as perhaps few have known Him in the history of mankind. She knew the meaning of the words: "This is life eternal, that they might know thee the only true God, and Jesus Christ, whom thou has sent." John 17:3. She personally accepted the promise of John 1:12, "But those who did welcome him, those who believed in his name, he authorized to become God's children."

As you read this volume you may well be drawn into Christ's presence, as have countless others. You may find Jesus standing before you with hands outstretched, saying: "I can answer your deepest personal and spiritual needs."

Steps to Christ, published in 100 languages, has sold more than 30 million copies globally. This edition represents perhaps the largest single printing of any religious book in history. The continued demand attests to its timelessness and the universality of its clear, direct, and simple message.

TO READ ONLINE GO TO:
http://www.seventh-day.org/steps-index.htm
OR EMAIL: For a free copy anywhere in the world:
sieketrooster@gmail.com

DEVOTIONAL BOOKS AVAILABLE
Dr Frank Gerald Steyn
sieketrooster@gmail.com

- ➤ *I'm OK; You're OK; GOD'S OK* (Devotional)
- ➤ *Bleeding Inside* (Depression and Burnout)
- ➤ *Sabbath of Grace* (Enjoying God's Freedom)
- ➤ *Revelation – Door of Hope* (Right Brain Bible)
- ➤ *The Greatest Secret Ever Told* (Jesus is the Key)
- ➤ *7 Bible Covenants* (God's Covenant People)

Each of these books is published, not as Dogmatic, Legalistic, or Academic and Objective theses, but as devotional books for prayer and thought. There are many books written by great prophetic scholars, available on the chronological, historical and prophetic teachings of Revelation. We also need to have some subjectivity in our lives. This includes the use our right brain. Read through the pages and chapters, meditate on the thoughts, and pray for your family, friends, community and your own heart and mind. Our prayer is that your life will be touched by the thoughts, stories, and Bible verities shared. These books are all available at AMAZON.COM.

Made in the USA
Charleston, SC
25 February 2017